SCHOLASTIC

YEAR IN SPORTS 2012

SCHOLASTIC INC.

NEW YORK • TORONTO • LONDON • AUCKLAND
SYDNEY • MEXICO CITY • NEW DELHI • HONG KONG

ISBN 978-0-545-33150-0

10 9 8 7 6 5 4 3 2 1 11 12 13 14 15

Printed in the U.S.A. 40
First edition, December 2011

Produced by Shoreline Publishing Group LLC

Due to the publication date, records, results, and statistics are current as of August 2011.

CONTENTS

INTRODUCTION

Tipoff: How a basketball game begins.

Books usually start with this: the introduction. Sports, on the other hand, start with all sorts of things: tip-offs, kickoffs, green flags, first pitches, starting horns, face-offs, first serves, even the opening of the gate in horse racing.

With the start of every sporting event comes the anticipation. You just never know what might happen. You might think you do . . . but you never know for sure. That's what makes sports so exciting and popular. Every event is fresh and original. Every game is live—not a repeat. After you've watched a movie or TV show once, you know how it ends. But every time an NBA game begins, you don't know how it ends. Every time you turn on an NFL game, it's a brand-new chance for something amazing to happen. Every time Shaun White zips down the vert ramp, he could end up as a hero . . . or on his backside. The NCAA basketball tournament starts with four No. 1 seeds . . . yet by the end, at least this year, they all might miss the final game. With sports, the beginning of something is just a tantalizing taste of the thrills still to come.

In the action-packed pages of this book, we've got tons of stories of beginnings and endings. From the first kickoff to the final whistle in the Super

Kick off to start a football game.

Bowl; from Opening Day to the last out of the World Series; from the first tip-off of the NBA season to the confetti-filled last game of the NBA Finals; from the Daytona 500 to the finale of the Chase for the Cup. (And that's not to mention sepak takraw, mud racing, and monster trucks!)

Of course, the athletes and teams doing all this beginning and ending are the reasons we really tune in to watch. Their stories from the past year are all inside. Look for these heroes and their championship teams: Aaron Rodgers and the Green Bay Packers; Tim Lincecum and the San Francisco Giants; Abby Wambach and the U.S. women's soccer team; Mark Ingram and Alabama; Kemba Walker and the Connecticut Huskies; Lionel Messi and FC Barcelona; Lauren Jackson and the Seattle Storm; and Dirk Nowitzki and the Dallas Mavericks.

Other athletes did their winning alone, superstars such as Jimmie Johnson, Novak Djokovic, Lindsey Vonn, Shaun White, Rory McIlroy, and Yani Tseng.

Now, of course, it's up to you to create your own beginning, when you turn the page and start your reading motor!

On your mark, get set . . . GO!

The green flag gets NASCAR's races rolling . . . fast!

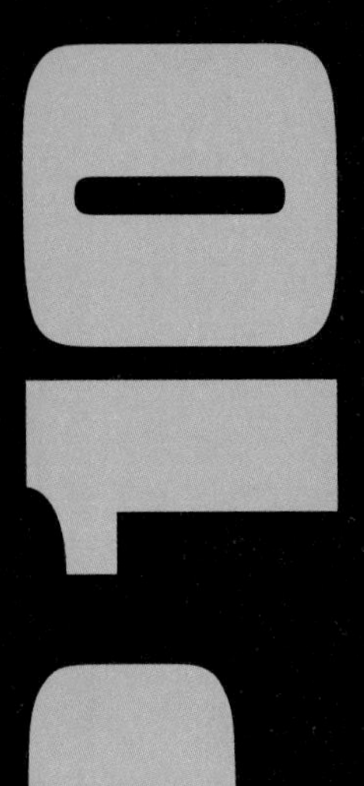

MOMENTS IN SPORTS

SEPTEMBER 2010 ▶ JULY 2011

Top 10. Los diez primeros. SIRSA DASA. Oberseite zehn. トップ10位

In whatever language you say it, it means the best of the best. We chose these languages (in order, they are English, Spanish, Hindi, German, and Japanese) because they all have something to do with the sports events we chose as our Top 10 for the past year.

Sports connects people from around the globe better than almost anything else. This past year saw several sports events that drew the world's attention. With real-time scoring and worldwide availability of video clips online, events such as the Cricket World Cup and the UEFA soccer championships can be followed minute by minute by billions of people.

Here in the U.S., the usual sports took center stage, but some of the heroes of those sports really stood out more than usual. Some of them got a spot on the list, too.

One event made the list not because it was so great, but because it affected so many fans. Anything that's in the news as much as the longest NFL lockout in history was really something to remember.

Tons of great moments and events didn't make the cut, but don't worry—all of the greatest sports moments from No. 11 to No. 199 are inside the rest of the book. Check out our choices here and get ready to argue why your favorites should have been included! That's part of the fun of sports, after all!

10
9
8
7
6
5
4
3
2...

10 *Though **Shaun White** has conquered snowboarding and the Olympics, gold in the skate vert had eluded him for four years. That changed with his awesome run at the 2011 X Games, as he showed off new tricks and dethroned reigning champ **Pierre Luc-Gagnon**.*

9 *After choking on the last day of the Masters,* ***Rory McIlroy*** *forged one of the greatest comebacks in sports. Just two months after his Masters disaster, he won the U.S. Open with the lowest score in the history of the tournament, and was the youngest U.S. Open winner ever.*

8 *You might not have seen this match, but more than a billion people around the world tuned in when India defeated Sri Lanka in the championship match of the Cricket World Cup. The event was played in India, so home fans got to cheer their heroes in person.*

7 *You'd be this happy, too, if you were **Lionel Messi**, the world's greatest soccer player, and you had just scored your second goal of the UEFA Champions League final. Messi led FC Barcelona to a 2–0 win over Manchester United to capture the title.*

6 *In April 2011, Texas Tech won its first NCAA women's basketball championship, but the real story of the event was that Connecticut lost! The Huskies first had their record 90-game winning streak snapped in November, then lost for the first time in three years in an NCAA tournament game to Notre Dame's women in green.*

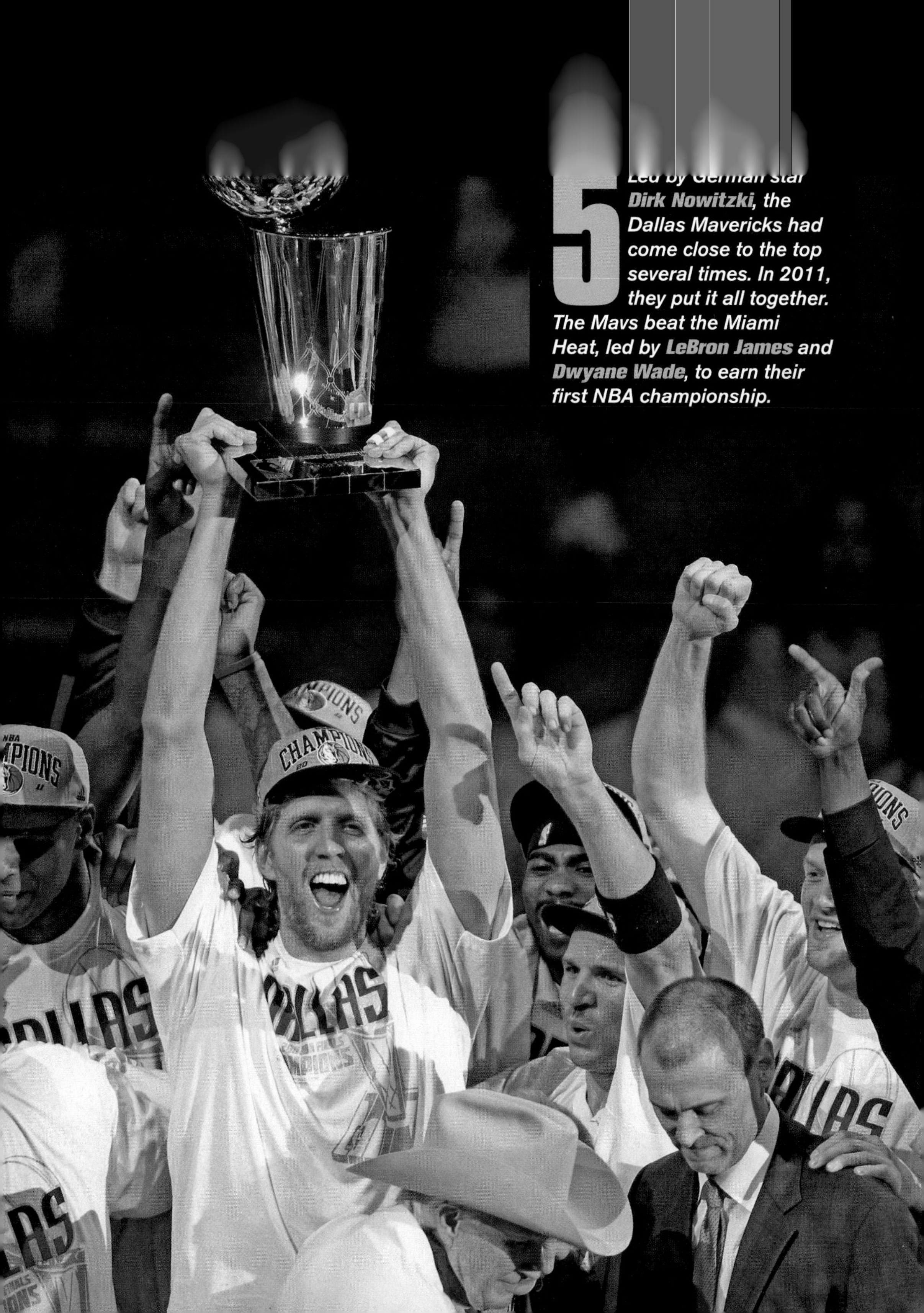

5 Led by German star **Dirk Nowitzki**, the Dallas Mavericks had come close to the top several times. In 2011, they put it all together. The Mavs beat the Miami Heat, led by **LeBron James** and **Dwyane Wade**, to earn their first NBA championship.

4

The best players come up big when their teams need them the most. ***Roy Halladay*** *did just that in October 2010. The Phillies ace became only the second pitcher ever to throw a no-hitter in the postseason, blanking the Reds, 4–0, in the NL Division Series.*

3 *Football fans learned another lesson about the importance of money and business in the world of sports when NFL owners locked out their players in March 2011.* ***DeMaurice Smith*** *(left) spoke for the players, NFL commissioner* ***Roger Goodell*** *for the owners. They talked for months about many issues relating to money in the sport. The longest NFL work stoppage ever finally ended on July 22.*

2 *In more exciting football news, the NFL's most successful franchise ended up back on top after the 2010 season. The Green Bay Packers won their 4th Super Bowl and 13th NFL championship, defeating the Pittsburgh Steelers, 31–25.*

pepsi
PACKERS
NORTH TEXAS 02.06.11
Wilson

WAMBACH
20

1

Until the final kicks of the 2011 Women's World Cup, ***Abby Wambach*** *of the U.S. was head and shoulders above the competition. Her last-minute goal vs. Brazil (pictured) was the most amazing sports moment of the year. Unfortunately, she and her teammates let two leads slip away in the final game and lost to Japan. That team (inset) gave the world, and its home country, still reeling from an earthquake and tsunami, a reason to celebrate the inspiring power of sports.*

NFL

NO. 12 IS NO. 1!
Green Bay Packers quarterback Aaron Rodgers signals touchdown after one of his team's scores in Super Bowl XLV. The Packers returned to the top of the NFL with a 31–25 victory over the Pittsburgh Steelers. Rodgers was named the Super Bowl MVP.

ONE CRAZY YEAR!

Fans watching the NFL in 2010 probably felt like they were on a roller coaster. Every week seemed to bring a new twist, turn, or change of direction. Snow was falling indoors (see page 34), losing teams were in the play-offs, and one player moved from prison to the field to become a star again. Thank goodness things got straightened out by Super Bowl time!

The early part of the season saw a string of strange plays by special teams. In one game, the San Diego Chargers had two punts blocked—after going eight years without any. In the same game, which was a loss to Seattle, they also gave up two kickoff-return TDs. The Miami Dolphins' special teams allowed a blocked punt, a blocked field goal returned for a touchdown, and a kickoff-return score in a 41–14 loss to New England.

Brady set a record for passing perfection.

The 2010 season didn't end happily for the Patriots' **Tom Brady**, as the Patriots were upset in the play-offs by the Jets (see page 26). However, the New England QB put on quite a show during the regular season. He threw 319 straight passes without an interception. That amazing streak topped the old mark of 308 by **Bernie Kosar**.

Another one of the biggest stories of the 2010 season was the comeback of Eagles quarterback **Michael Vick**. He had been one of the most exciting players in the NFL before he had to leave the game for more than three years. Vick was sent to prison for his part in a dogfighting scandal. Many thought that his career was over. However, Vick finished his prison term and the NFL decided to let him back in if he followed the rules. Vick had several remarkable games (see page 30) and made a lot of fantasy football team owners happy. By putting his mistakes behind him, Vick has remade his life . . . and his football career.

The Atlanta Falcons continued their rise as one of the league's best teams, thanks in large part to QB **Matt Ryan** and WR **Roddy White**. In the AFC, Kansas City showcased RB **Jamaal Charles** and WR **Dwayne Bowe**, and was the surprise AFC West champ. On the other hand, the Dallas Cowboys won only one game in their fabulous new stadium.

The play-offs were the scene of several upsets. Seattle, the NFC West champions, was the first team ever to earn a play-off spot with a losing record (7–9). In the wild-card round, they stunned the defending Super Bowl champs, beating the New Orleans Saints in a 41–36 shoot-out. In the AFC, the Jets beat both the Colts and the Patriots, sending star QBs **Peyton Manning** and Brady to the showers early.

Classic NFL order was restored in the Super Bowl, however (see page 24). The Packers kept the Steelers from earning yet another Super Bowl win while bringing home the Lombardi Trophy to Green Bay.

Ryan led Atlanta to a division title.

2010 Final Regular-Season Standings

AFC EAST	W	L
New England	14	2
N.Y. Jets	11	5
Miami	7	9
Buffalo	4	12

AFC NORTH	W	L
Pittsburgh	12	4
Baltimore	12	4
Cleveland	5	11
Cincinnati	4	12

AFC SOUTH	W	L
Indianapolis	10	6
Jacksonville	8	8
Houston	6	10
Tennessee	6	10

AFC WEST	W	L
Kansas City	10	6
San Diego	9	7
Oakland	8	8
Denver	4	12

NFC EAST	W	L
Philadelphia	10	6
N.Y. Giants	10	6
Dallas	6	10
Washington	6	10

NFC NORTH	W	L
Chicago	11	5
Green Bay	10	6
Detroit	6	10
Minnesota	6	10

NFC SOUTH	W	L
Atlanta	13	3
New Orleans	11	5
Tampa Bay	10	6
Carolina	2	14

NFC WEST	W	L
Seattle	7	9
St. Louis	7	9
San Francisco	6	10
Arizona	5	11

THE PACK IS BACK!

Somewhere in football heaven, **Vince Lombardi** was smiling down on Dallas on February 6. That's because the team that the famous coach led to five NFL titles had earned the trophy named after him. The Green Bay Packers won their all-time record 13th NFL championship with a 31–25 win over Pittsburgh in Super Bowl XLV.

In the first Super Bowl played in the new Cowboys Stadium (home of the world's largest video screen!), fans of these two great NFL teams packed the seats. Once the game got under way beneath the dome, Green Bay QB **Aaron Rodgers** was hot enough to melt all the ice in Wisconsin! He wrapped up an amazing postseason streak of success, throwing three TD passes and earning MVP honors.

Collins (36) scored a key TD on an interception return.

PACKERS POWER!

The years in which the Packers were NFL champions:

2010
1996
1967
1966
1965
1962
1961
1944
1939
1936
1931
1930
1929

The Packers became only the second team to win the Super Bowl as the lowest-seeded play-off team. That underdog spirit was part of the Packers' entire year, as they battled several early-season injuries to key players. That continued even into the Super Bowl itself, after star cornerback **Charles Woodson** had to leave the game in the first half with a shoulder injury.

Rodgers is all smiles holding the trophy.

The Steelers came into the game with six Super Bowl titles of their own, the most of any team (most of the Packers' championships came in the years before the Super Bowl). The Steelers hoped that their great defense would be able to stop Rodgers's hot hand, but it was the Packers' defense that made the difference early, with a first-quarter "pick six" (interception return for a touchdown) by **Nick Collins** pushing the score to 14–0. After a Pittsburgh field goal, Rodgers threw another TD to **Greg Jennings** for a 21–3 lead.

> ***"Green Bay is where the trophy belongs. As long as the Packers have lived, it's going to be great to bring that back."***
>
> — GREEN BAY LB **A. J. HAWK**

In the fourth quarter, Jennings's second TD catch and a field goal by Packers K **Mason Crosby** put the game out of the Steelers' reach. Green and gold confetti showered down on the joyous Packers as they eagerly grabbed the trophy from NFL Commissioner Roger Goodell.

Adding another page to their championship legend, Packers coach **Mike McCarthy** had the team measured for Super Bowl rings—the night *before* the game! Planning ahead like that might have been bad luck for some teams, but with Lombardi smiling down on them, the Pack was back, rings, trophy, and all.

BOX SCORE

Green Bay	**14**	**7**	**0**	**10**
Pittsburgh	**0**	**10**	**7**	**7**

GB–Nelson 29 pass from Rodgers (Crosby kick)
GB–Collins 27 interception return (Crosby kick)
PIT–FG Suisham 33
GB–Jennings 21 pass from Rodgers (Crosby kick)
PIT–Ward 8 pass from Roethlisberger (Suisham kick)
PIT–Mendenhall 8 run (Suisham kick)
GB–Jennings 8 pass from Rodgers (Crosby kick)
PIT–Wallace 25 pass from Roethlisberger (Suisham kick)
GB–FG Crosby 23

2010 POSTSEASON

Mark Sanchez led the Jets to a pair of upset victories.

Wild Card

NFC **Seahawks 41, Saints 36**

The defending Super Bowl champs lost to the 7–9 Seahawks in one of the biggest upsets in NFL play-off history!

Packers 21, Eagles 16

A strong Green Bay defense bottled up the explosive **Michael Vick**.

AFC **Jets 17, Colts 16**

Another Super Bowl favorite fell in an upset as the Jets continued their amazing postseason success.

Ravens 30, Chiefs 7

K.C.'s fairy-tale season came to a quick end, thanks to the crushing Baltimore defense.

Divisional

NFC **Bears 35, Seahawks 24**

Seattle ran out of magic against Chicago.

Packers 48, Falcons 21

A trio of **Aaron Rodgers** TD passes keyed an offensive show.

AFC **Jets 28, Patriots 24**

There they go again! The surprising Jets kept finding a way to win over the top teams.

Steelers 31, Ravens 24

The Steelers and Big Ben ended up on top.

Matt Hasselbeck was a big part of the Seahawks' win.

Conference Championships

NFC **Packers 21, Bears 14**

A big interception return by Green Bay's **B. J. Raji** was the key to the Pack's NFC title.

AFC **Steelers 24, Jets 16**

A fumble-return TD and a goal-line stand gave Pittsburgh the AFC crown.

AWARD WINNERS

NFL MVP

Tom Brady, QB, New England

This was an easy pick, considering Brady's new record for passes without an interception (319), plus the Patriots' NFL-best 14–2 record. The vote was also unanimous for the first time.

OFFENSIVE PLAYER OF THE YEAR

Tom Brady, QB, New England

This was the second time Brady has won both awards; he last did the double in 2007.

DEFENSIVE PLAYER OF THE YEAR

Troy Polamalu, S, Pittsburgh

The long-haired Tasmanian devil of a defender edged out linebacker **Clay Matthews** of the Packers to win his first postseason honor.

OFFENSIVE ROOKIE OF THE YEAR

Sam Bradford, QB, St. Louis

The former Heisman Trophy winner led the Rams to six more wins in 2010 than they had in 2009, plus set NFL rookie records for attempts and completions.

DEFENSIVE ROOKIE OF THE YEAR

Ndamukong Suh, DT, Detroit

With 10 sacks, Suh showed that the Lions made the right choice with the No. 2 overall pick of the draft.

WALTER PAYTON NFL MAN OF THE YEAR

Madieu Williams, S, Minnesota

For his work in public health as well as his help in his homeland of Sierra Leone, Williams earned this award thanks to his great community service.

Bradford was the No. 1 draft pick in 2010 . . . good move, Rams!

THE LEADERS

1,616 RUSHING YARDS
Arian Foster, Houston

111.0 PASSER RATING
Tom Brady, New England

36 TOUCHDOWN PASSES
Tom Brady, New England

4,710 PASSING YARDS
Philip Rivers, San Diego

115 RECEPTIONS
Roddy White, Atlanta

1,448 RECEIVING YARDS
Brandon Lloyd, Denver

143 POINTS
David Akers, Philadelphia

18 TOUCHDOWNS
Arian Foster, Houston

15.5 SACKS
DeMarcus Ware, Dallas

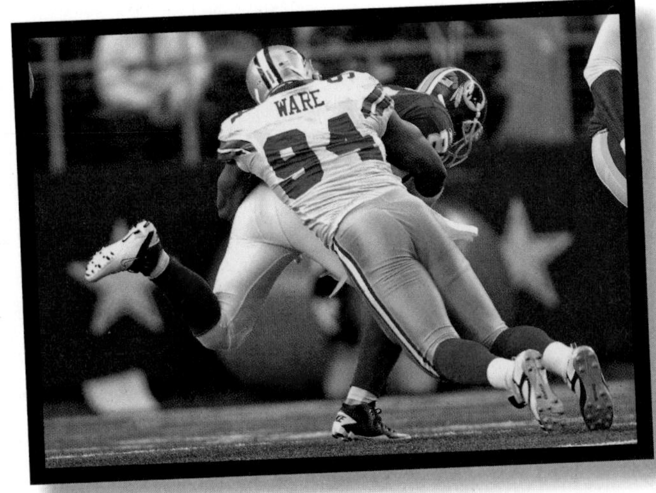

33 FIELD GOALS
Josh Brown, St. Louis
Sebastian Janikowski, Oakland

8 INTERCEPTIONS
Ed Reed, Baltimore

175 TACKLES
Jerod Mayo, New England

45.5 PUNTING AVERAGE
Donnie Jones, St. Louis

MILESTONES AND RECORDS

◀◀◀ * **Devin Hester** set a new NFL record with his 14th special teams TD.

* The Chicago Bears became the first NFL team to reach 700 wins!

* **Tony Gonzalez** became the only tight end ever with more than 1,000 career catches and more than 12,000 receiving yards. ▶▶▶

* **Randy Moss** and **Terrell Owens** became the second and third wide receivers (after **Jerry Rice**) with more than 150 career touchdown catches.

* New England's **Bill Belichick** became the first coach to lead his team to four 14-win seasons.

2010: BIG DAYS!

Woo-hoo! Scobee scampers after his big kick.

What a Finish!

The Jacksonville Jaguars won a game on October 3 thanks to one of the longest game-winning field goals ever. Jaguars kicker **Josh Scobee** set a career record—by 8 yards—with a final-play 59-yard field goal that beat the Colts, 31–28.

Phabulous Philly

The Eagles and Giants battled for a play-off spot in a week-15 game that featured an NFL first for an ending. The Giants grabbed a 31–10 lead with just about half of the fourth quarter left. But in another display of his miraculous comeback ability, **Michael Vick** led the Eagles to 21 points to tie the game. He threw for a pair of touchdowns and ran for a third amid the furious rally.

With the game tied and just seconds left, the Eagles forced the Giants to punt. Punter **Matt Dodge** was told to kick the ball out of bounds to force overtime. Instead, his punt landed in the hands of the talented **DeSean Jackson**. Jackson burst past the startled Giants, racing 65 yards for the score. It was the first time that an NFL game ended that way. Jackson had scored the first-ever walk-off punt return.

Game over! Jackson heads for the final six.

Jones makes a game-tying catch.

A Comeback, and a Letdown

The Houston Texans faced long odds in their comeback attempt against Baltimore. They trailed, 28–7, in the fourth quarter and were facing an awesome Baltimore defense. Texans QB **Matt Schaub** ignored all that and put together an amazing quarter.

Schaub led a team-record 99-yard drive that ended with a touchdown pass. The Texans' defense held, giving Schaub one more chance. He engineered another great drive, this one for 95 yards! With just 21 seconds left, **Andre Johnson** caught a TD pass from Schaub to make the score 28–26. Schaub then hit **Jacoby Jones** on a two-point conversion to force overtime.

Unfortunately, Schaub had emptied his magic bag. Just a few plays into overtime, he threw an interception that was returned by Baltimore's **Josh Wilson** for the game-winning touchdown.

Monday Madness

Eagles QB **Michael Vick** put on a show for the ages in a Monday night game against the Redskins. Vick accounted for six touchdowns as the Eagles pounded the Redskins, 59–28. Vick threw four TD passes while rushing for two more scores. He became the first QB in NFL history to pass for 300 yards and rush for 50, while also notching those six scores.

Vick is just about unstoppable in a Monday night game in D.C.

STORIES FROM THE FIELD

"I had my mom, my aunt, and two cousins in the stands. The first ball went to my mom, the second ball went to my aunt, and the next thing you knew, everybody had a ball."

— **DeANGELO HALL**, AFTER HIS FOUR-PICK DAY

QUICK PICKS

Washington Redskins cornerback **DeAngelo Hall** had a big game against the Bears. He picked off four passes in the game! He was the nineteenth player to snag that many, but he was only the first to do so in 10 years.

COMEBACK KINGS

In 1992, the Buffalo Bills set an NFL record by coming back from 38 points to win a play-off game over the Houston Oilers, 41–38. On November 21, 2010, they called on that long-ago magic to beat the Bengals. In the second half, the Bills trailed, 28–7, but then scored 35 points to rally to a surprising 49–31 win.

HOT STARTS

Cleveland QB **Colt McCoy** had a tough road ahead of him. In one three-game stretch, he and the Browns faced a trio of quarterbacks who had each won a Super Bowl: Pittsburgh's **Ben Roethlisberger**, New England's **Tom Brady**, and New Orleans's **Drew Brees**. But after losing to Big Ben and the Steelers, McCoy led his team to upset wins over both the Patriots and the Saints. The Saints also lost to another surprising rookie QB, **Max Hall** of the Cardinals, who beat them, 30–20. Better yet for Arizona, yet another rookie QB, **John Skelton**, helped the Cardinals beat Denver!

OAKLAND'S BIG DAY

The Raiders and Broncos have played a lot of big games in their history. The two teams first faced off in the old AFL and have continued their rivalry in the AFC West. In week 7, the Raiders came up with the biggest score in the team's 50-year history, piling up 59 points to the Broncos' 14. Running back **Darren McFadden** had four touchdowns in the scoring binge.

I Think I Can, I Think I Can . . .

Months later, New England's **Dan Connolly** is probably still panting after this play. The Packers tried a short kickoff play against the Pats in a late December game. Connolly somehow ended up with the ball, and 71 yards later, the 313-pound guard had the longest kickoff return ever by an NFL lineman.

A Snowstorm—Indoors!

TV cameras captured something amazing at the Metrodome in Minnesota . . . and it wasn't a great play in a Vikings game. A few days before the team was set to play in their home dome, a huge snowstorm caused part of the stadium roof to cave in! The video showed a huge mound of snow pouring through the broken roof onto the empty field.

Minnesota's December 12 game against the Giants had to be moved to December 13 at the nearby University of Minnesota. The roof couldn't be fixed the next week, so the Vikings had to play outdoors again on December 20. They got clobbered by the Bears, 40–14.

Finally, on December 28, snow hammered the Vikes again. Before a planned Monday night game at Philadelphia, a snowstorm made travel near the stadium impossible. The game was postponed and became the first Tuesday night game in the NFL since 1946.

WORLD'S BIGGEST KICKER

Defensive tackle **Ndamukong Suh** of Detroit normally gets near a ball only if it's being held by the running back he's just squashed. In a game against the Jets in November, however, the Lions called on the 307-pounder for another role. Kicker **Jason Hanson** was hurt, and Suh was tabbed to try a point-after-touchdown kick. Suh missed the kick, and the Lions ended up losing in overtime, 23–20.

In other PAT news, Buffalo's **Rian Lindell** missed one. Why is that news? The Bills' kicker hadn't missed an extra point in 321 straight tries!

One Shoe Short

On Thanksgiving Day, the Jets' **Brad Smith** was in such a hurry to get to his postgame turkey that he ran right out of his shoe! Midway through a kickoff return, Smith lost one of his cleats. He didn't need it, however, and completed an 89-yard TD return. Among players with at least 25 returns, Smith's 28.6-yard average led the NFL.

2011 Hall of Fame Class

Welcome these outstanding stars to the Pro Football Hall of Fame:

- **Richard Dent**, DE
- **Marshall Faulk**, RB
- **Chris Hanburger**, LB
- **Les Richter**, LB
- **Deion Sanders**, CB/KR
- **Shannon Sharpe**, TE

Also inducted was **Ed Sabol**, the founder of NFL Films.

"Neon Deion" created excitement on every play.

GOOD-BYE, BRETT

Keep this page. This will be the page you talk to your grandkids about. You'll be able to say you saw **Brett Favre** in action. The great quarterback retired (for good this time!) after the 2010 season as the NFL's all-time leader in every important passing category (see box). He also created a reputation for toughness and leadership that will be hard to match.

Favre started his career with a single season in Atlanta but moved to Green Bay in 1992. For the next 16 seasons, he was the unquestioned leader of the Pack. In only 1 of those 16 seasons did Green Bay have a losing record, while 9 times he led them to 10 or more victories.

FAVRE'S CAREER HIGHLIGHTS

- Led NFL in TD passes four times
- Named to 11 Pro Bowls
- NFL MVP 1995, 1996, 1997
- MVP of Super Bowl XXXI

FAVRE'S ALL-TIME NFL RECORDS

- 10,169 pass attempts
- 6,300 completions
- 71,838 passing yards
- 508 touchdown passes
- 336 interceptions
- 525 times being sacked

The high points of his Packers career came in 1996, when he brought the Vince Lombardi Trophy back to Green Bay with a win in Super Bowl XXXI. His exuberant dash down the field, helmet held high in triumph (left), is how many of his fans will remember him.

Though he played one year for the Jets and two for the Vikings to close out his career, he will be most remembered for his fantastic time with Green Bay.

Here's one more number: 297. That's how many consecutive NFL games Favre started, coming back from injuries big and small to answer the call. He was dependable, tough, talented . . . and a winner. Keep this page; you'll be glad you got to see him play.

2011 DRAFT

Even with the lockout of players (see below), the NFL Draft was held in April 2011. Here are the top 10 picks.

PICK	PLAYER, POSITION	NFL TEAM	SCHOOL
1	Cam Newton, QB	Panthers	Auburn
2	Von Miller, LB	Broncos	Texas A&M
3	Marcell Dareus, DT	Bills	Alabama
4	A. J. Green, WR	Bengals	Georgia
5	Patrick Peterson, CB	Cardinals	LSU
6	Julio Jones, WR	Falcons	Alabama
7	Aldon Smith, DE	49ers	Missouri
8	Jake Locker, QB	Titans	Washington
9	Tyron Smith, T	Cowboys	USC
10	Blaine Gabbert, QB	Jaguars	Missouri

THE LOCKOUT

The biggest news in the NFL was not the Packers' return to the top. It was the lockout. Until March 12, 2011, the NFL and its players had an agreement that controlled how much money from the teams went to the players. Without a new agreement, the league and its players could not officially work together. The NFL chose to "lock out" the players while both sides worked on a new agreement. That meant that players couldn't practice, and coaches couldn't talk to players.

It was a very unpleasant time for fans, players, and coaches. Finally, in July, after it had become the longest "time-out" in NFL history, the league and its players came to an agreement. Fans of all ages learned again this off-season: Sports aren't just about games . . . they're also about business.

THE ENVELOPE, PLEASE

Cam Newton had a pretty good year. He led his Auburn team to the national championship. He won the Heisman Trophy as the top player in the country. And he was the No. 1 draft pick at the 2011 NFL Draft. Newton was not a big surprise, but the two other QBs picked in the top 10 (see list) were not expected. Most experts figured only Newton has the best chance to start in 2011.

FOR THE RECORD

Super Bowl Winners

GAME	SEASON	WINNING TEAM	LOSING TEAM	SCORE	SITE
XLV	2010	**Green Bay**	Pittsburgh	**31–25**	Dallas
XLIV	2009	**New Orleans**	Indianapolis	**31–17**	South Florida
XLIII	2008	**Pittsburgh**	Arizona	**27–23**	Tampa
XLII	2007	**N.Y. Giants**	New England	**17–14**	Glendale, Ariz.
XLI	2006	**Indianapolis**	Chicago	**29–17**	South Florida
XL	2005	**Pittsburgh**	Seattle	**21–10**	Detroit
XXXIX	2004	**New England**	Philadelphia	**24–21**	Jacksonville
XXXVIII	2003	**New England**	Carolina	**32–29**	Houston
XXXVII	2002	**Tampa Bay**	Oakland	**48–21**	San Diego
XXXVI	2001	**New England**	St. Louis	**20–17**	New Orleans
XXXV	2000	**Baltimore**	N.Y. Giants	**34–7**	Tampa
XXXIV	1999	**St. Louis**	Tennessee	**23–16**	Atlanta
XXXIII	1998	**Denver**	Atlanta	**34–19**	South Florida
XXXII	1997	**Denver**	Green Bay	**31–24**	San Diego
XXXI	1996	**Green Bay**	New England	**35–21**	New Orleans
XXX	1995	**Dallas**	Pittsburgh	**27–17**	Tempe, Ariz.
XXIX	1994	**San Francisco**	San Diego	**49–26**	South Florida
XXVIII	1993	**Dallas**	Buffalo	**30–13**	Atlanta
XXVII	1992	**Dallas**	Buffalo	**52–17**	Pasadena
XXVI	1991	**Washington**	Buffalo	**37–24**	Minneapolis

GAME	SEASON	WINNING TEAM	LOSING TEAM	SCORE	SITE
XXV	1990	**N.Y. Giants**	Buffalo	**20–19**	Tampa
XXIV	1989	**San Francisco**	Denver	**55–10**	New Orleans
XXIII	1988	**San Francisco**	Cincinnati	**20–16**	South Florida
XXII	1987	**Washington**	Denver	**42–10**	San Diego
XXI	1986	**N.Y. Giants**	Denver	**39–20**	Pasadena
XX	1985	**Chicago**	New England	**46–10**	New Orleans
XIX	1984	**San Francisco**	Miami	**38–16**	Stanford
XVIII	1983	**L.A. Raiders**	Washington	**38–9**	Tampa
XVII	1982	**Washington**	Miami	**27–17**	Pasadena
XVI	1981	**San Francisco**	Cincinnati	**26–21**	Pontiac, Mich.
XV	1980	**Oakland**	Philadelphia	**27–10**	New Orleans
XIV	1979	**Pittsburgh**	Los Angeles	**31–19**	Pasadena
XIII	1978	**Pittsburgh**	Dallas	**35–31**	Miami
XII	1977	**Dallas**	Denver	**27–10**	New Orleans
XI	1976	**Oakland**	Minnesota	**32–14**	Pasadena
X	1975	**Pittsburgh**	Dallas	**21–17**	Miami
IX	1974	**Pittsburgh**	Minnesota	**16–6**	New Orleans
VIII	1973	**Miami**	Minnesota	**24–7**	Houston
VII	1972	**Miami**	Washington	**14–7**	Los Angeles
VI	1971	**Dallas**	Miami	**24–3**	New Orleans
V	1970	**Baltimore**	Dallas	**16–13**	Miami
IV	1969	**Kansas City**	Minnesota	**23–7**	New Orleans
III	1968	**N.Y. Jets**	Baltimore	**16–7**	Miami
II	1967	**Green Bay**	Oakland	**33–14**	Miami
I	1966	**Green Bay**	Kansas City	**35–10**	Los Angeles

ROAR OF THE TIGERS

Delirious LSU players and their fans celebrate the Tigers' second-chance, come-from-behind victory over Tennessee *(see page 46)**. It was a fantastic finish in a season full of fantastic finishes—all the way to the BCS title game.*

COLLEGE FOOTBALL

Oregon was No. 1 at the start of the BCS title game, but Auburn ended up on top.

WHO'S NO. 1?

The Auburn Tigers beat the Oregon Ducks, 22–19, in the BCS National Championship Game for 2010. That capped a wild and crazy college football season in which it was anybody's guess which teams would wind up in the championship game.

Defending champ Alabama began the season as the top team in the Associated Press rankings, but the Crimson Tide was upset at South Carolina in early October. That made Ohio State No. 1, but the Buckeyes lost at Wisconsin in their first game atop the rankings. So Oklahoma took over, but the Sooners lost, too (at Missouri), in their first game as No. 1.

Then it was Auburn's turn at the top, but Oregon was so impressive that the Ducks vaulted over the Tigers and became No. 1. Meanwhile, Boise State fans argued that their undefeated team deserved a chance.

In the end, Auburn and Oregon both remained undefeated going into the title game, and most college football fans felt that those

Auburn coach Gene Chizik hoists the trophy.

FINAL 2010 TOP 10

(From the Associated Press)

1. **Auburn**
2. **TCU**
3. **Oregon**
4. **Stanford**
5. **Ohio State**
6. **Oklahoma**
7. **Wisconsin**
8. **LSU**
9. **Boise State**
10. **Alabama**

were the best teams. So the BCS system—designed to pit the top two teams in the final game—worked, right? Well, maybe not. Fans of the TCU Horned Frogs would certainly disagree. The Horned Frogs finished undefeated themselves and beat an excellent Wisconsin team in the Rose Bowl. TCU's defense just might have been good enough to stop the wild offenses of Auburn and Oregon. But the Horned Frogs never got the chance to show it on the field. So cries for a college football play-off still aren't likely to end . . . until there's a play-off!

Award Winners

College football's best team featured college football's best player in 2010—that doesn't happen as often as you might think. Auburn quarterback **Cam Newton** won the Heisman Trophy as the top player. He became just the third player (but the second in a row) since the BCS was formed in 1998 to win the Heisman and the national title in the same year. Here were the major college football award winners for 2010:

HEISMAN TROPHY (BEST PLAYER)
Cam Newton, Auburn

DOAK WALKER AWARD (RUNNING BACK)
LaMichael James, Oregon

DAVEY O'BRIEN AWARD (QUARTERBACK)
Cam Newton, Auburn

FRED BILETNIKOFF AWARD (WIDE RECEIVER)
Justin Blackmon, Oklahoma State

JOHN MACKEY AWARD (TIGHT END)
D. J. Williams, Arkansas

OUTLAND TROPHY (INTERIOR LINEMAN)
Gabe Carimi, Wisconsin

VINCE LOMBARDI/ROTARY AWARD (LINEMAN)
Nick Fairley, Auburn

CHUCK BEDNARIK AWARD (DEFENSIVE PLAYER)
Patrick Peterson, LSU

BRONKO NAGURSKI AWARD (DEFENSIVE PLAYER)
Da'Quan Bowers, Clemson

DICK BUTKUS AWARD (LINEBACKER)
Von Miller, Texas A&M

JIM THORPE AWARD (DEFENSIVE BACK)
Patrick Peterson, LSU

LOU GROZA AWARD (KICKER)
Dan Bailey, Oklahoma State

2009 MAJOR BOWL GAMES

BCS National Championship Game

Auburn 22, Oregon 19

Fiesta Bowl

Oklahoma 48, Connecticut 20

Orange Bowl

Stanford 40, Virginia Tech 12

◀◀◀ Rose Bowl

TCU 21, Wisconsin 19

Sugar Bowl

Ohio State 31, Arkansas 26

MORE FOOTBALL TROPHIES

Football Championship Subdivision

Eastern Washington 20, Delaware 19

Division II

Minnesota Duluth 20, Delta State 17 ▶▶▶

Division III

Wisconsin-Whitewater 31, Mount Union 21

WAR EAGLE!

When the 13–0 Auburn Tigers ("War Eagle!" is their rallying cry) took on the 12–0 Oregon Ducks in the BCS National Championship Game in January 2011, all the experts agreed: It was going to be one heck of a shoot-out. The Tigers entered the game averaging 42.7 points per game; the Ducks were even better at 49.3 points. Their offense often snapped the ball only seconds after the previous play had ended. Their scoring drives were lightning quick.

Auburn featured the Heisman Trophy winner in quarterback **Cam Newton**; Oregon had the nation's touchdown leader in running back **LaMichael James**. Both teams liked to play at a crazy pace. The score figured to look more like a basketball game's than a football game's. So, naturally . . . it was a defensive struggle!

Actually, both teams piled up a lot of yards. But both sides also had trouble scoring points because the defenses came up with big plays at the right time. In the end, Auburn won, 22–19, when **Wes Byrum** kicked a 19-yard field goal as time ran out. The experts can at least be happy with the fact that it was a great offensive play that set up the winning field goal. From Auburn's 40-yard line, running back **Michael Dyer** ran for what appeared to be a short gain. But he rolled on top of his would-be tackler, never touching the ground. He got up and kept going for a 37-yard gain to the Ducks' 23. The Tigers eventually reached the 1-yard line before kicking the short field goal to win it.

Auburn star DT Nick Fairley (90) helped stop the Ducks.

CHALK TALK

The Outsiders

The "Big Six" is the nickname for the major conferences: the Atlantic Coast, Big 12, Big East, Big Ten, Pac-12, and Southeastern. The winners of those conferences get automatic berths in the BCS bowls. Non-BCS schools have a disadvantage because they don't get an automatic berth for winning their conference. However, in 2010, TCU, from the Mountain West Conference, went undefeated. The Horned Frogs beat No. 4 Wisconsin in the Rose Bowl to finish the year No. 2.

Caution: One Way!

Chicago's Wrigley Field, the home of baseball's Cubs, is the second-oldest stadium in baseball. But there used to be football at Wrigley, too. Northwestern decided it would be a cool idea to play a home game against Illinois there. However, when the football field was laid out, the east end zone nearly butted up against the outfield wall. The solution: Every offensive snap went toward the west end zone. Every time there was a change of possession, the teams switched sides! Illinois won this slightly odd game, 48–27.

Frantic Finish

The biggest comeback in 2010 was LSU's victory over Tennessee (pictured on pages 40–41). The

Tigers trailed, 14–10, late in the game. LSU drove to the 2-yard line in the final seconds. On the next play, the quarterback wasn't ready and the snap went past him. However, two minutes later, an official signaled a penalty on Tennessee! Too many players on the field. One more play for LSU. The Tigers ran it in for the winning TD. Final score: 16–14.

Double Trouble

Quarterbacks throw the ball and running backs run it. Well, at Nevada, QBs throw the ball *and* run it. Wolfpack quarterback **Colin Kaepernick** finished his career in 2010 as the only player in NCAA Division I history to pass for 10,000 yards and rush for 4,000 yards. He became the third player to rush for 20 TDs and pass for 20 TDs in the same season.

Stanford's Throwback Player

Stanford's **Owen Marecic** went old school in 2010. He became the first Division I player in decades to start regularly on both offense (at fullback) and defense (linebacker). Those are two of the most physically tough positions, too, and he did it for one of the best teams in the country. (Stanford went 12–1 in 2010.) In a victory against Notre Dame early in the season, Marecic ran 1 yard for a touchdown in the fourth quarter. Then, on Notre Dame's first play following the kickoff, he intercepted a pass and returned it 20 yards for another touchdown. Two touchdowns in 13 seconds!

TOP FIVE GAMES

Nevada 34, Boise State 31 (OT)

1 If not for this game, Boise State would have made its claim for a national championship. The Broncos entered the game ranked No. 3 with a 10–0 record in 2010 and riding a 24-game winning streak. Nevada had lost only once in 11 games. Boise State jumped out to a 24–7 lead at halftime before Nevada chipped away. The Wolfpack pulled even on a touchdown with 17 seconds left. Boise State missed short field-goal tries on the final play of regulation and the first series of overtime. Then Nevada made a field goal to claim the big win.

Auburn 28, Alabama 27

2 The Tigers' hopes for a national championship appeared to be over when they fell behind the defending-champion Crimson Tide, 24–0, in the second quarter. Alabama had never lost a game in which it led by as many as 24 points. But eventual Heisman Trophy winner **Cam Newton** rallied Auburn by passing for three touchdowns and running for another. Auburn took the lead early in the fourth quarter and its defense held on from there.

Oklahoma 47, Oklahoma State 41

3 In the game that put them in the Big 12 title match, the Sooners were the last team standing. The game was tied, 24–24, before a wild fourth quarter that featured four field goals and four touchdowns, including long-distance scores of 86, 89, and 77 yards. The last of those came on a long pass from **Landry Jones** to **James Hanna**.

Michigan 69, Illinois 67 (three OTs)

4 Check that score—no, this is not the basketball section! This game featured 1,237 yards of total offense, including 676 by the winning Wolverines. There were 49 points scored in the second quarter alone, and the score was tied, 45–45, after four quarters. Then came a high-scoring overtime to decide the winner.

Michigan State 34, Notre Dame 31 (OT)

5 The game was tied, 28–28, at the end of regulation. The Irish kicked a field goal in overtime to go ahead. Then Michigan State lined up for a tying field goal. Instead, holder **Aaron Bates** took the snap and tossed a game-winning, 28-yard TD pass to **Charlie Gantt**. Surprise!

BY THE NUMBERS

Leaders in key stat categories:

39 TOUCHDOWN PASSES
Bryant MONIZ, Hawaii ▶▶▶

5,040 PASSING YARDS
Bryant MONIZ, Hawaii

1,731 RUSHING YARDS
LaMichael JAMES, Oregon

131 RECEPTIONS
Ryan BROYLES, Oklahoma

1,889 RECEIVING YARDS
Greg SALAS, Hawaii

24 TOUCHDOWNS
LaMichael JAMES, Oregon

28 FIELD GOALS
Josh JASPER, LSU

183 TACKLES
◀◀◀ **Luke KUECHLY**, Boston College

CONFERENCE CHAMPS

◀◀◀ ATLANTIC COAST **Virginia Tech**

The Hokies started out as possible national champs. Then they opened the season with losses to Boise State and James Madison. That put an end to that! They rallied to win 11 games in a row and beat Florida State in the ACC title game.

BIG EAST **Connecticut**

Most experts figured that Pittsburgh or West Virginia, not Connecticut, would win the Big East. But the Huskies ended with five wins in a row to do just that!

BIG TEN **Wisconsin, Ohio State, Michigan State**

These three schools all had powerful squads. Each lost only one game before the bowls. So technically, they all shared the Big Ten title for 2010. The conference's automatic BCS berth, though, went to the highest-ranked school. That was Wisconsin.

BIG 12 **Oklahoma**

Traditional powerhouses Oklahoma and Nebraska squared off in the title game before the Cornhuskers bolted to the Big Ten for the 2011 season. The Sooners sent their longtime rivals away by rallying from a 17–0 deficit to win, 23–20.

PAC-10 **Oregon** ▶▶▶

The Ducks' point-a-minute (well, almost) offense carried them to their second Pac-10 title in a row. Oregon's only real competition for the title came from Stanford. Both teams were undefeated when they played in Eugene in October. The Cardinal jumped to a 21–3 lead in the first quarter, but it was all Ducks after that. Final score: Oregon 51, Stanford 32.

SOUTHEASTERN **Auburn**

West Division champ Auburn put its undefeated season on the line against East champ South Carolina in the SEC title game. South Carolina already had a string of upsets to its credit, including a win over defending national champ Alabama. Auburn won in a rout (56–17) to punch its ticket to the national championship game.

A LOOK AHEAD

CONFERENCE SHAKE-UP

There are lots of changes in college football for the 2011 season. Several top conferences have added new teams.

* The Pac-10 is now the Pac-12 after adding Colorado and Utah.
* The Big Ten had 11 teams but it has 12 now after adding Nebraska (which used to be in the Big 12).
* The Big 12 is still the Big 12 but it is down to 10 teams, believe it or not.

In 2012, the Big East will add TCU, even though that school is in Texas. And Boise State has moved to the Mountain West. Got all that? Don't worry, there won't be a test!

WILL OKLAHOMA BE OK?

Which team will survive the BCS jumble to win the 2011 season? One team on almost everybody's list of candidates is Oklahoma (right). The Sooners will return most of their first- and second-string players on both offense and defense from 2010—and that team went 12–2! Out west, Oregon's offense looks to be awesome again. Meanwhile, Alabama and LSU will try to continue the Southeastern Conference's streak of five consecutive victories in the BCS title game.

As you look ahead to 2011, remember this: The undefeated 2010 champ was Auburn. And at the start of that season, the Tigers were way down at No. 22!

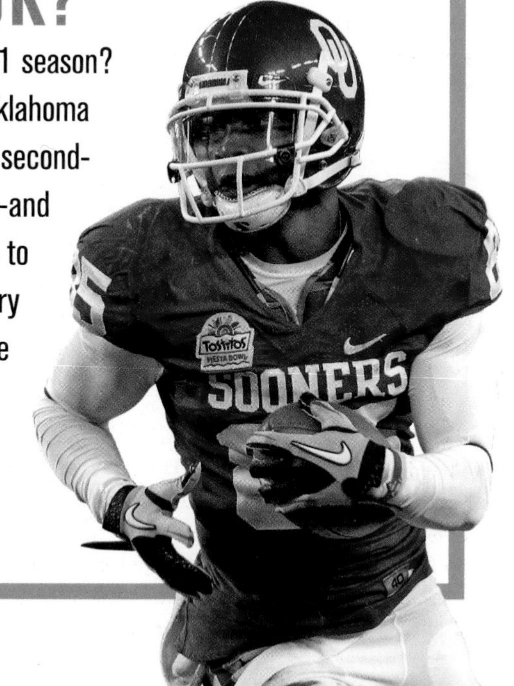

WE'RE NO. 1

These are the teams that have finished at the top of the Associated Press's final rankings since the poll was first introduced in 1936.

SEASON	TEAM	RECORD
2010	**Auburn**	14–0
2009	**Alabama**	14–0
2008	**Florida**	13–1
2007	**LSU**	10–2
2006	**Florida**	13–1
2005	**Texas**	13–0
2004	**USC**	13–0
2003	**USC**	12–1
2002	**Ohio State**	14–0
2001	**Miami**	12–0
2000	**Oklahoma**	13–0
1999	**Florida State**	12–0
1998	**Tennessee**	13–0
1997	**Michigan**	12–0
1996	**Florida**	12–1
1995	**Nebraska**	12–0
1994	**Nebraska**	13–0
1993	**Florida State**	12–1
1992	**Alabama**	13–0
1991	**Miami**	12–0
1990	**Colorado**	11–1–1
1989	**Miami**	11–1
1988	**Notre Dame**	12–0
1987	**Miami**	12–0
1986	**Penn State**	12–0
1985	**Oklahoma**	11–1
1984	**Brigham Young**	13–0
1983	**Miami**	11–1
1982	**Penn State**	11–1
1981	**Clemson**	12–0
1980	**Georgia**	12–0
1979	**Alabama**	12–0
1978	**Alabama**	11–1
1977	**Notre Dame**	11–1
1976	**Pittsburgh**	12–0
1975	**Oklahoma**	11–1
1974	**Oklahoma**	11–0
1973	**Notre Dame**	11–0

SEASON	TEAM	RECORD
1972	**USC**	12–0
1971	**Nebraska**	13–0
1970	**Nebraska**	11–0–1
1969	**Texas**	11–0
1968	**Ohio State**	10–0
1967	**USC**	10–1
1966	**Notre Dame**	9–0–1
1965	**Alabama**	9–1–1
1964	**Alabama**	10–1
1963	**Texas**	11–0
1962	**USC**	11–0
1961	**Alabama**	11–0
1960	**Minnesota**	8–2
1959	**Syracuse**	11–0
1958	**LSU**	11–0
1957	**Auburn**	10–0
1956	**Oklahoma**	10–0
1955	**Oklahoma**	11–0
1954	**Ohio State**	10–0
1953	**Maryland**	10–1
1952	**Michigan State**	9–0
1951	**Tennessee**	10–1
1950	**Oklahoma**	10–1
1949	**Notre Dame**	10–0
1948	**Michigan**	9–0
1947	**Notre Dame**	9–0
1946	**Notre Dame**	8–0–1
1945	**Army**	9–0
1944	**Army**	9–0
1943	**Notre Dame**	9–1
1942	**Ohio State**	9–1
1941	**Minnesota**	8–0
1940	**Minnesota**	8–0
1939	**Texas A&M**	11–0
1938	**Texas Christian**	11–0
1937	**Pittsburgh**	9–0–1
1936	**Minnesota**	7–1

BOWL CHAMPIONSHIP SERIES
NATIONAL CHAMPIONSHIP GAMES

College football (at its highest level) is one of the few sports that doesn't have an on-field play-off to determine its champion. In the 1998 season, the NCAA introduced the Bowl Championship Series (BCS), which pits the top two teams in the title game according to a complicated formula that takes into account records, polls, and computer rankings. At the end of the regular season, the No. 1 and No. 2 teams meet in a championship game, usually during the first week of January after all the major bowl games have been played. Here are the results of all the BCS title games.

SEASON	SCORE	SITE
2010	**Auburn 22, Oregon 19**	GLENDALE, AZ
2009	**Alabama 37, Texas 21**	PASADENA, CA
2008	**Florida 24, Oklahoma 14**	MIAMI, FL
2007	**LSU 38, Ohio State 24**	NEW ORLEANS, LA
2006	**Florida 41, Ohio State 14**	GLENDALE, AZ
2005	**Texas 41, USC 38**	PASADENA, CA
2004	**USC 55, Oklahoma 19**	MIAMI, FL
2003	**LSU 21, Oklahoma 14**	NEW ORLEANS, LA
2002	**Ohio State 31, Miami 24**	TEMPE, AZ
2001	**Miami 37, Nebraska 14**	PASADENA, CA
2000	**Oklahoma 13, Florida State 2**	MIAMI, FL
1999	**Florida State 46, Virginia Tech 29**	NEW ORLEANS, LA
1998	**Tennessee 23, Florida State 16**	TEMPE, AZ

FEAR THE BEARD!
San Francisco Giants closer Brian Wilson, as famous for his jet-black beard as for his fastball, starts the celebration after his team won the 2010 World Series. The Giants beat the Texas Rangers in five games.

SAN FRANCISCO
SAN FRANCISCO
A2000

A GIANT SUCCESS!

A few years ago, everyone in baseball was talking about home runs . . . *huge batches* of home runs. Baseballs were flying out of the yard like skyrockets on the Fourth of July. The game has changed, however. Power is down, and pitchers are on top.

The early 2010 season saw a pair of perfect games (and another near-perfect game) and a couple of no-hitters. Reds lefty **Aroldis Chapman** threw the fastest pitch ever recorded: 105 mph! Plus, by the end of the season, the Diamondbacks had set a dismal record. Pitchers struck out 1,529 Arizona batters in 2010, the most ever in one season. Then, in the postseason, **Roy Halladay** did something that hadn't been done since 1956—see page 58 to find out what! (Great pitching performances continued in the first half of 2011, when **Francisco Liriano** and **Justin Verlander** each had no-hitters.)

Tim Lincecum's pitching led the Giants.

C. J. Wilson of Texas was the AL champion's ace.

The 2010 World Series showed the trend of pitching power. The San Francisco Giants didn't have any big sluggers. Young catcher **Buster Posey** was a rising star and veteran **Aubrey Huff** had a career year, but the Giants won it all thanks to an amazing set of starting pitchers. It was San Francisco's first World Series title since they moved to the West Coast in 1958.

San Francisco was not even in the play-off picture until September, in fact. However, to end the regular season, San Francisco's starters reeled off an amazing streak. In 18 straight games in late September, they gave up no more than three earned runs in each game.

2010 FINAL STANDINGS

AL EAST	
Rays	96–66
Yankees	95–67
Red Sox	89–73
Blue Jays	85–77
Orioles	66–96

AL CENTRAL	
Twins	94–68
White Sox	88–74
Tigers	81–81
Indians	69–93
Royals	67–95

AL WEST	
Rangers	90–72
Athletics	81–81
Angels	80–82
Mariners	61–101

NL EAST	
Phillies	97–65
Braves	91–71
Marlins	80–82
Mets	79–83
Nationals	69–93

NL CENTRAL	
Reds	91–71
Cardinals	86–76
Brewers	77–85
Astros	76–86
Cubs	75–87
Pirates	57–105

NL WEST	
Giants	92–70
Padres	90–72
Rockies	83–79
Dodgers	80–82
Diamondbacks	65–97

On the final day of the regular season, **Jonathan Sanchez** shut down the Padres, 3–0, giving the Giants the NL West title.

In the American League, the Texas Rangers were trying something new, too: pitching. The Rangers have a tradition of sluggers dating back many years. Under new owner **Nolan Ryan**, a Hall of Fame pitcher, the hurlers took a bigger role. Texas pitchers were better than they had ever been, and the Rangers ended up in the World Series for the first time.

The Giants got the clutch hits and won their first World Series since 1951.

The NL Wins One!

In 2010, for the first time since 1996, the National League won the All-Star Game! With the win, they earned home-field advantage in the World Series. Only a tie in 2002 had prevented the American League from having a run of 13 straight victories. In 2010, Atlanta catcher **Brian McCann** doubled home three runs in the seventh inning, while NL pitchers bottled up a strong AL lineup. The Giants should send McCann a thank-you note, since they used that home field to win the World Series!

2010 POSTSEASON

DIVISION SERIES

AL: Yankees 3, Twins 0
The Yankees made it nine straight play-off wins over the Twins, sweeping their series.

AL: Rangers 3, Rays 2
Texas beat Tampa Bay for its first play-off series win ever.

NL: Phillies 3, Reds 0
Philadelphia's ace pitchers, led by **Roy Halladay** with his no-hitter in Game 1 (see box), shut down the Reds, who had led the NL in average, home runs, and RBI.

NL: Giants 3, Braves 1
Behind great pitching and clutch hitting, the Giants beat the Braves in four games. The series ended Atlanta manager **Bobby Cox**'s Hall of Fame career on the bench, while giving the Giants their first NLCS berth since 2002.

CHAMPIONSHIP SERIES

AL: Rangers 4, Yankees 1
The Rangers outscored New York, 38–19. Texas outfielder **Josh Hamilton** had three homers and was named the LCS MVP. The Rangers won their first American League championship ever, 49 years after they started play as the Washington Senators in 1961.

NL: Giants 4, Phillies 2
Great pitching overcame great hitting—again. The Giants' pitching staff, led by **Tim Lincecum** and **Matt Cain**, held the powerful Philly bats in check. In the deciding Game 6, the Giants' bull pen pitched seven innings of one-run ball. Third baseman **Juan Uribe** won Game 4 with a ninth-inning sacrifice fly, and his home run put the Giants ahead in the clinching game, 3–2.

HALLADAY GOES FOR TWO

With his no-hitter in Game 1 of the NLDS, **Roy Halladay** of the Phillies became the first player since **Nolan Ryan** in 1973 with two no-nos in one season. Halladay had thrown a perfect game on May 29. Speaking of perfect games, Halladay joined **Don Larsen**, who threw his perfecto in Game 5 of the 1956 World Series, as the only pitchers with no-hitters in postseason play.

2010 WORLD SERIES

One thing everyone knew before this World Series started: No matter which team won, the result would make baseball history!

GAME 1: Giants

Boom, boom, boom! The Giants put up the second-most runs ever in a Game 1, highlighted by **Juan Uribe**'s three-run homer, winning a slugfest, 11–7. A game that started as a pitcher's showcase—**Cliff Lee** vs. **Tim Lincecum**—turned into a batter's battle. Also, **Elvis Andrus** became the first Elvis ever to appear in a World Series.

GAME 2: Giants

Matt Cain of the Giants dominated the Rangers' bats, shutting them down for seven-plus innings, while his teammates racked up 9 more runs. The 20 runs by the Giants in the first two games was the most ever to start a Series.

GAME 3: Rangers

Back in Texas, the Rangers must have enjoyed the home cooking, winning, 4–2, behind rookie **Mitch Moreland**'s three-run homer and the pitching of **Colby Lewis**. The Giants couldn't answer Moreland's second-inning shot, and the home team won the first World Series game ever played in Texas.

Fear the Beard! Wilson with the Series trophy.

GAME 4: Giants

Madison Bumgarner came one inning away from being first rookie to pitch a postseason shutout since 1948. With help from black-bearded closer **Brian Wilson**, the Giants did blank Texas. The Rangers' mighty bats disappeared, while the Giants pounded a pair of homers: a two-run shot by **Aubrey Huff** and a solo job by rookie sensation **Buster Posey**.

GAME 5: Giants

A three-run homer by **Edgar Renteria** provided all the runs that ace pitcher Lincecum needed to clinch the Giants' first World Series title since 1954. After hitting only three dingers in the regular season, Renteria hit two in the series and earned the MVP Award. Lincecum outpitched another postseason star, Lee, throwing seven innings and allowing only three hits, while striking out 10 Rangers. The Giants' powerful pitching proved to be decisive in shutting down the Rangers' big bats.

WORLD SERIES MVP: SS EDGAR RENTERIA, Giants: .412, 2 HR, 6 RBI

2010 AWARD WINNERS

MOST VALUABLE PLAYER

AL: **Josh Hamilton**
RANGERS

NL: **Joey Votto** ▶▶▶
REDS

CY YOUNG AWARD

AL: **Felix Hernandez**
MARINERS

NL: **Roy Halladay**
PHILLIES

ROOKIE OF THE YEAR

AL: **Neftali Perez**
RANGERS

NL: **Buster Posey**
GIANTS

RELIEF PITCHER OF THE YEAR

AL: **Rafael Soriano**
RAYS

NL: **Heath Bell**
PADRES

MANAGER OF THE YEAR

AL: **Ron Gardenhire**
TWINS

NL: **Bud Black**
PADRES

HANK AARON AWARD

(voted by fans for top offensive player)

◀◀◀ AL: **Jose Bautista**
BLUE JAYS

NL: **Joey Votto**
REDS

ROBERTO CLEMENTE AWARD

(for community service)

Tim Wakefield
RED SOX

2010 STATS LEADERS

AL HITTING LEADERS

HOME RUNS: 54
Jose Bautista, BLUE JAYS

RBI: 126
Miguel Cabrera, TIGERS

AVERAGE: .359
Josh Hamilton, RANGERS

STOLEN BASES: 68
Juan Pierre, WHITE SOX ▶▶▶

HITS: 214
Ichiro Suzuki, MARINERS

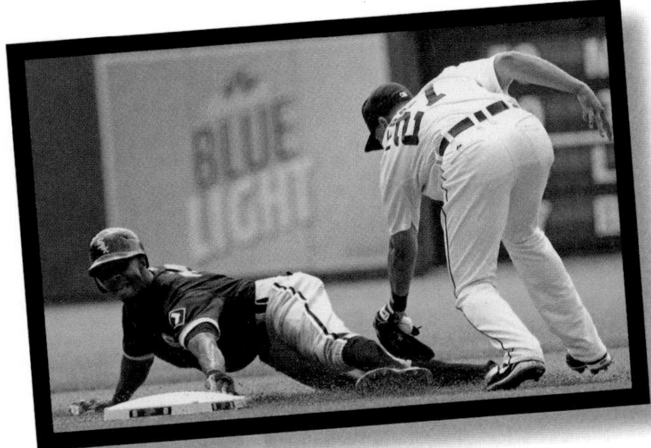

HITS: 197
Carlos Gonzalez, ROCKIES

NL HITTING LEADERS

HOME RUNS: 42
Albert Pujols, CARDINALS

RBI: 118
Albert Pujols, CARDINALS

AVERAGE: .336
Carlos Gonzalez, ROCKIES

STOLEN BASES: 52
Michael Bourn, ASTROS

AL PITCHING LEADERS

WINS: 21
CC Sabathia, YANKEES

SAVES: 45
Rafael Soriano, RAYS

ERA: 2.27
Felix Hernandez, MARINERS

STRIKEOUTS: 233
Jered Weaver, ANGELS

NL PITCHING LEADERS

WINS: 21
Roy Halladay, PHILLIES

SAVES: 48
Brian Wilson, GIANTS

ERA: 2.30
◀◀◀ **Josh Johnson,** MARLINS

STRIKEOUTS: 231
Tim Lincecum, GIANTS

AROUND THE BASES: 2010

Jose "Wow"tista! ▸▸▸

In his first six Major League seasons, **Jose Bautista** hit 59 homers in 575 games. In 2010, he put that all behind him. The Blue Jays left fielder blasted a big-league-leading 54 homers in 161 games! He was the first player to top 50 homers since **Alex Rodriguez** had 54 in 2007. Amazingly, he hit all but one of his homers to left or center fields. Talk about a dead-pull hitter! Bautista proved he was no one-season fluke by reaching 20 homers in his first 48 games of 2011, too. Why the power surge? Bautista credited a new swing he built with the help of hitting coach **Dwayne Murphy**. Here's a good guess: Coach Murphy got a really nice Christmas present from Bautista!

Ichiro Does It Again

Seattle's amazing outfielder **Ichiro Suzuki** set a Major League record with his 10th straight season with 200 hits. Since he's only been in the majors 10 years, that's even more amazing. Suzuki, of course, came over from Japan, where he remains an enormous superstar. He also won his 10th Gold Glove for defensive excellence, tying a record for outfielders.

QUICK HITS

- ✸ **Carlos Gonzalez** slammed a homer to complete the sixth cycle in Rockies history.
- ◂ **Alex Rodriguez** became the youngest player in history (34) to reach 600 career homers. He also became the first player with 100 RBI in 14 seasons.
- ✸ At 47, **Jamie Moyer** of the Phillies became the oldest player ever to throw a complete-game shutout.
- ✸ **Trevor Hoffman** became the first closer to reach 600 saves.

Thanks, Guys

While Astros pitcher **Bud Norris** got dressed for pregame practice, his teammates pulled an awesome prank on him. They got his car, drove it onto the warning track in the outfield, and painted a huge target on it using shaving cream. When Bud went out to the field, he saw his car . . . and all the baseballs that were heading toward it! After a few laughs, he drove it off the field and back to the lot . . . a bit dinged, but ready for the road.

Four in a Row

Baseball announcers call two homers in a row "back-to-back jacks." On August 11, 2010, Arizona's radio guys had to come up with something new. For only the fourth time in Major League history, a team hit *four* home runs in a row. The Diamondbacks' fearsome foursome were **Adam LaRoche**, **Miguel Montero**, **Mark Reynolds**, and **Stephen Drew**.

Bruuuuuce!

It's every player's dream: Hit a home run that gives your team a championship. In most of those dreams, the homer comes in the bottom of the ninth, too. On September 28, 2010, Cincinnati outfielder **Jay Bruce** saw his boyhood dreams come true. He smacked a walk-off homer that broke a 2–2 tie with the Astros and clinched the NL Central title for the Reds. It was only the fifth time that a walk-off homer has sent a team to the postseason.

Best in Baseball?

Albert Pujols is continuing to break all-time records. The Cardinals' slugging first baseman had 42 homers in 2010. That made him the first player ever with 10 straight 30-homer seasons to start a career. One of those homers was his 400th overall, too. He capped off a typically awesome season by finishing second in the NL MVP voting. He has won the award three times and has never finished a season lower than fourth in the voting. Wow!

AROUND THE BASES: 2011

✷ A pair of Rangers got the defending AL champs off to a fast start. **Ian Kinsler** and **Nelson Cruz** became the first teammates in baseball history to each homer in their team's first three games.

◀◀◀ ✷ Baseball of the future? On Science Day in Philadelphia, a one-armed, three-wheeled robot named PhillieBot threw out the first pitch in a game against Milwaukee. The pitch fell short of home plate, so the technology still needs some work!

✷ Talk about fast starts! The Angels' **Jered Weaver** went 6–0 in April. He became the first pitcher ever with four wins by April 18!

✷ Drama in Cleveland! In July, the Indians trailed by three runs in the bottom of the ninth. Then **Travis Hafner** hit a walk-off grand slam.

Jeter's 3000!

Derek Jeter got his 3,000th career hit on July 9 . . . and he got it in style. The Yankees shortstop and captain hit a home run for No. 3000. But that's not all—he got four more hits in the game! Jeter became the 28th player in MLB history to reach 3,000 hits. He was the second ever to hit a homer for the milestone hit. At 37, he's still young enough that other hit records are out there for him to chase. (The all-time record? 4,256 by **Pete Rose**.)

Verlander Goes for Two

Justin Verlander threw the second no-hitter of his career on May 8. Verlander relies on a powerful fastball, and he was throwing so well in this game that he hit 100 mph in the ninth inning! The Tigers' righty walked just one Toronto batter while striking out four, and Detroit won, 9–0.

The Twins' **Francisco Liriano** also had a no-hitter earlier in the same week. His was not quite as pretty as Verlander's, however. The Minnesota lefty struggled with his control, walking six batters and needing 123 pitches to close it out. However, when the White Sox did hit the ball, it went right at the Twins' defense.

✷ **Ben Zobrist** had a pretty good day on April 28. The Tampa Bay utility man was only the fourth player since 1920 with 7 hits and 10 RBI in one doubleheader!

✷ The May 26 Reds-Phillies game was still tied when outfielder **Wilson Valdez** was called on to pitch the 19th inning. He held the Reds scoreless, and Philly won in the bottom of the inning. Valdez was only the third position player ever to earn a pitching victory.

✷ In a game in August, the Yankees trailed the A's, 7–1. They came back in a big way! The Bronx Bombers set a major-league record by blasting three grand slams in the game! They won, 22–9.

✷ **Justine Siegal** became the first woman to throw batting practice to Major Leaguers when she pitched to the Cleveland Indians during spring training in Arizona. ▶▶▶

✷ **Prince Fielder** smacked a three-run homer and the NL earned its second straight All-Star Game win. The game featured great pitching by the NL, led by **Roy Halladay** and **Cliff Lee**. The W gave the NL home-field advantage in the World Series . . . again!

TOP 2011 YOUNG STARS

Alexi OGANDO, RANGERS SP

With victories in his first six decisions, Ogando showed that Texas made the right move by taking him from the bull pen and putting him in the starting rotation.

◀◀◀ Michael PINEDA, MARINERS SP

A power pitcher like his teammate Felix Hernandez, Pineda will be among the favorites for Rookie of the Year.

◀◀◀ Mark TRUMBO, ANGELS 1B

A surprise starter in April, Trumbo showed a lot of pop and figures to be an Angels regular for many years.

Starlin CASTRO, CUBS SS

With speed and range, Castro caught fans' eyes early in 2011. He also got a spot on the cover of *Sports Illustrated*. Not bad for a 21-year-old!

Jordan WALDEN, ANGELS RP

Walden started the season as the closer of the future for the Angels. The future came quickly. By the second week of the season, he was using his great fastball to save games in Anaheim.

Freddie FREEMAN, BRAVES 1B

With Atlanta veterans like Chipper Jones available for him to learn from, Freeman's in a great place to develop his smooth, left-handed, home-run swing.

THE HALL 2011

Baseball's Hall of Fame welcomed a pair of baseball lifers in 2011, along with one of the top infielders of his era.

Roberto Alomar ▶▶▶

Baseball was a family affair in the Alomar house. Roberto's father, Sandy, played in the Majors for 15 years. His brother, Sandy Jr., was a catcher for seven teams in 20 years. Second baseman Roberto was the best of the Alomars. The 1988 AL Rookie of the Year went on to win 10 Gold Gloves in a 17-year career. He had a .300 career average and eight seasons with 30 or more stolen bases. A 12-time All-Star, he helped the Blue Jays win the 1992 and 1993 World Series.

Bert Blyleven

Fourteen years is a long time to wait for the "call from the Hall." But it was worth it to this excellent pitcher. Blyleven won 287 games in 22 seasons with five teams. He spent the most time with the Twins. His 60 career shutouts are ninth all-time, while his 3,701 strikeouts are fifth. Blyleven won at least 15 games in 10 seasons. Trivia time: He was born in the Netherlands; his full name is Rik Aalbert Blyleven.

Pat Gillick

Gillick never wore a Major League uniform, but he owns three World Series rings. As a general manager, he helped build championship teams in Toronto and Philadelphia. He also created play-off teams in Baltimore and Seattle. Gillick has been in baseball for more than 50 years.

2011 WORLD SERIES: A PREDICTION

By the time you read this, you may have already watched the World Series. We're going out on a limb, but we're going to put our guesses here for who you watched. See how well we did!

★ **Boston Red Sox** OVER **Philadelphia Phillies** ★

WORLD SERIES WINNERS

YEAR	WINNER	RUNNER-UP	SCORE*
2010	San Francisco Giants	Texas Rangers	4-1
2009	New York Yankees	Philadelphia Phillies	4-2
2008	Philadelphia Phillies	Tampa Bay Rays	4-1
2007	Boston Red Sox	Colorado Rockies	4-0
2006	St. Louis Cardinals	Detroit Tigers	4-1
2005	Chicago White Sox	Houston Astros	4-0
2004	Boston Red Sox	St. Louis Cardinals	4-0
2003	Florida Marlins	New York Yankees	4-2
2002	Anaheim Angels	San Francisco Giants	4-3
2001	Arizona Diamondbacks	New York Yankees	4-3
2000	New York Yankees	New York Mets	4-1
1999	New York Yankees	Atlanta Braves	4-0
1998	New York Yankees	San Diego Padres	4-0
1997	Florida Marlins	Cleveland Indians	4-3
1996	New York Yankees	Atlanta Braves	4-2
1995	Atlanta Braves	Cleveland Indians	4-2
1993	Toronto Blue Jays	Philadelphia Phillies	4-2
1992	Toronto Blue Jays	Atlanta Braves	4-2
1991	Minnesota Twins	Atlanta Braves	4-3
1990	Cincinnati Reds	Oakland Athletics	4-0
1989	Oakland Athletics	San Francisco Giants	4-0
1988	Los Angeles Dodgers	Oakland Athletics	4-1
1987	Minnesota Twins	St. Louis Cardinals	4-3
1986	New York Mets	Boston Red Sox	4-3
1985	Kansas City Royals	St. Louis Cardinals	4-3

YEAR	WINNER	RUNNER-UP	SCORE*
1984	Detroit Tigers	San Diego Padres	4-1
1983	Baltimore Orioles	Philadelphia Phillies	4-1
1982	St. Louis Cardinals	Milwaukee Brewers	4-3
1981	Los Angeles Dodgers	New York Yankees	4-2
1980	Philadelphia Phillies	Kansas City Royals	4-2
1979	Pittsburgh Pirates	Baltimore Orioles	4-3
1978	New York Yankees	Los Angeles Dodgers	4-2
1977	New York Yankees	Los Angeles Dodgers	4-2
1976	Cincinnati Reds	New York Yankees	4-0
1975	Cincinnati Reds	Boston Red Sox	4-3
1974	Oakland Athletics	Los Angeles Dodgers	4-1
1973	Oakland Athletics	New York Mets	4-3
1972	Oakland Athletics	Cincinnati Reds	4-3
1971	Pittsburgh Pirates	Baltimore Orioles	4-3
1970	Baltimore Orioles	Cincinnati Reds	4-1
1969	New York Mets	Baltimore Orioles	4-1
1968	Detroit Tigers	St. Louis Cardinals	4-3
1967	St. Louis Cardinals	Boston Red Sox	4-3
1966	Baltimore Orioles	Los Angeles Dodgers	4-0
1965	Los Angeles Dodgers	Minnesota Twins	4-3
1964	St. Louis Cardinals	New York Yankees	4-3
1963	Los Angeles Dodgers	New York Yankees	4-0
1962	New York Yankees	San Francisco Giants	4-3
1961	New York Yankees	Cincinnati Reds	4-1
1960	Pittsburgh Pirates	New York Yankees	4-3

* Score is represented in games played.

YEAR	WINNER	RUNNER-UP	SCORE*
1959	Los Angeles Dodgers	Chicago White Sox	4-2
1958	New York Yankees	Milwaukee Braves	4-3
1957	Milwaukee Braves	New York Yankees	4-3
1956	New York Yankees	Brooklyn Dodgers	4-3
1955	Brooklyn Dodgers	New York Yankees	4-3
1954	New York Giants	Cleveland Indians	4-0
1953	New York Yankees	Brooklyn Dodgers	4-2
1952	New York Yankees	Brooklyn Dodgers	4-3
1951	New York Yankees	New York Giants	4-2
1950	New York Yankees	Philadelphia Phillies	4-0
1949	New York Yankees	Brooklyn Dodgers	4-1
1948	Cleveland Indians	Boston Braves	4-2
1947	New York Yankees	Brooklyn Dodgers	4-3
1946	St. Louis Cardinals	Boston Red Sox	4-3
1945	Detroit Tigers	Chicago Cubs	4-3
1944	St. Louis Cardinals	St. Louis Browns	4-2
1943	New York Yankees	St. Louis Cardinals	4-1
1942	St. Louis Cardinals	New York Yankees	4-1
1941	New York Yankees	Brooklyn Dodgers	4-1
1940	Cincinnati Reds	Detroit Tigers	4-3
1939	New York Yankees	Cincinnati Reds	4-0
1938	New York Yankees	Chicago Cubs	4-0
1937	New York Yankees	New York Giants	4-1
1936	New York Yankees	New York Giants	4-2
1935	Detroit Tigers	Chicago Cubs	4-2
1934	St. Louis Cardinals	Detroit Tigers	4-3
1933	New York Giants	Washington Senators	4-1
1932	New York Yankees	Chicago Cubs	4-0

YEAR	WINNER	RUNNER-UP	SCORE*
1931	St. Louis Cardinals	Philadelphia Athletics	4-3
1930	Philadelphia Athletics	St. Louis Cardinals	4-2
1929	Philadelphia Athletics	Chicago Cubs	4-1
1928	New York Yankees	St. Louis Cardinals	4-0
1927	New York Yankees	Pittsburgh Pirates	4-0
1926	St. Louis Cardinals	New York Yankees	4-3
1925	Pittsburgh Pirates	Washington Senators	4-3
1924	Washington Senators	New York Giants	4-3
1923	New York Yankees	New York Giants	4-2
1922	New York Giants	New York Yankees	4-0
1921	New York Giants	New York Yankees	5-3
1920	Cleveland Indians	Brooklyn Dodgers	5-2
1919	Cincinnati Reds	Chicago White Sox	5-3
1918	Boston Red Sox	Chicago Cubs	4-2
1917	Chicago White Sox	New York Giants	4-2
1916	Boston Red Sox	Brooklyn Dodgers	4-1
1915	Boston Red Sox	Philadelphia Phillies	4-1
1914	Boston Braves	Philadelphia Athletics	4-0
1913	Philadelphia Athletics	New York Giants	4-1
1912	Boston Red Sox	New York Giants	4-3
1911	Philadelphia Athletics	New York Giants	4-2
1910	Philadelphia Athletics	Chicago Cubs	4-1
1909	Pittsburgh Pirates	Detroit Tigers	4-3
1908	Chicago Cubs	Detroit Tigers	4-1
1907	Chicago Cubs	Detroit Tigers	4-0
1906	Chicago White Sox	Chicago Cubs	4-2
1905	New York Giants	Philadelphia Athletics	4-1
1903	Boston Red Sox	Pittsburgh Pirates	5-3

Note: 1904 not played because NL-champion Giants refused to play; 1994 not played due to MLB work stoppage.

COLLEGE BASKETBALL

A TROPHY FOR A&M!
After two consecutive women's basketball titles for Connecticut, most people thought they'd make it three in a row. Texas A&M's Aggies had other ideas, however, and they won their first national championship after UConn fell in the semifinals to Notre Dame.

NO.1
NATIONAL CHAMPIONS
2011 NCAA WOMEN'S BASKETBALL

HOOP DREAMS

The 2010–11 college basketball season was like riding a roller coaster in an elevator on a seesaw! From beginning to end, it was a topsy-turvy, up-and-down season packed with upsets, comebacks, surprises, and, finally, a historic Final Four. After the coaster stopped, the last team standing had finished ninth in its conference in the regular season. That's right—ninth!

San Diego State and BYU battled in the west.

A handful of schools always seem to be in the national championship picture—teams such as Duke, North Carolina, Michigan, Kentucky, and others. In 2010–11, however, once the games got started, reputations went out the window. Teams jumped in and out of the Top 25 like it was a game of musical chairs. Earning the weekly No. 1 ranking was a pretty good way to guarantee that you'd lose soon; half a dozen teams made the top spot only to lose soon after.

The first major surprises came out west . . . the Mountain West Conference, to be exact. No team from that group has ever been ranked No. 1, and none has made the Final Four. But in 2010–11, two teams from the Mountain West were regularly among the Top 10. BYU was led by superscorer **Jimmer Fredette**, the national player of the year (see page 77), while San Diego State boasted a huge lineup that dominated in the paint. The conference battles between these two teams were awesome, with BYU coming out on top twice—the only losses San Diego State had until the NCAA tournament started.

> ***"Who was better prepared than us to play this game today at home? This was our time. This was our moment to have a breakthrough."***
>
> — ST. JOHN'S COACH **STEVE LAVIN** AFTER HIS TEAM UPSET DUKE

When all the ups and downs were over, Connecticut ended up on top!

Meanwhile, in the Big East, Connecticut, a two-time champion in the past decade, entered the season unranked. Though the Huskies ended up winning all their nonconference games, they finished ninth in the Big East. St. John's, which had not had a winning team for more than a decade, was a surprising conference standout, finishing fifth. Notre Dame returned to a high level of play, finishing second.

Another traditional powerhouse, Duke, was ranked first for a long time during the season but was upset several times. In the Midwest, Ohio State was picked by many experts as the best team in the country. Then the Buckeyes lost to Wisconsin, in a game that they led by as many as 15 points!

On one wild weekend in late January, 14 teams ranked in the Top 25 lost. Ten of those losses came against teams that were not ranked at all. The biggest win was by St. John's over Duke. The 15-point margin was the worst loss by the Blue Devils in 15 seasons to an unranked team.

By the time the NCAA tournament rolled around, no one knew what would happen. With all the upsets, a team needed a hot streak to make it to the top. Connecticut found that heat. The Huskies won five games in five days to win the Big East tournament, an impressive feat all by itself.

In the NCAA tournament, they continued their roll, sweeping into the Sweet Sixteen and then beating San Diego State to make the Final Four. There, the Huskies beat Kentucky and Butler (see page 74) to capture the championship. (Butler itself was a pretty big story, a "small school" returning to the championship game, where they had lost in 2010.) The convincing win gave Connecticut its third national title since 1999 (they also won in 2004 and 2007).

FINAL AP TOP 10

1. Connecticut
2. Butler
3. Kentucky
4. Kansas
5. Ohio State
6. VCU
7. Duke
8. North Carolina
9. Arizona
10. Florida

The amazing tournament run by VCU surprised and delighted college hoops fans.

MARCH MADNESS!

The 2011 NCAA men's championship tournament will be remembered for three letters: V, C, and U. Those stand for Virginia Commonwealth University, the No. 11 seed that nearly made it to the top of the NCAA.

The second thing people will remember might be called the other Cinderella. In 2010, little Butler University came within a barely missed three-point shot of upsetting Duke and winning the national title. No one expected them to get another chance. Surprise! They became the first team since Florida in 2001 to reach to the national title game two years in a row. Unfortunately, Butler also became the first team since Michigan in 1993 to lose two in a row! Butler was a No. 8 seed, but it wasn't alone in crashing the Final Four party. Thanks to all the upsets, the Final Four contained no No. 1 or No. 2 seeds for the first time in NCAA tournament history.

First and Second Round

The Southwest Region was Upset City. Five out of eight lower-ranked teams won their first games in upsets. The biggest was Morehead State (13th seed) over Louisville (4). VCU (11) knocked off Big East power Georgetown (6).

Kemba Walker (15) led UConn to its third NCAA title and then cut down the net in celebration (below).

In the Southeast, Butler's second-round win over Pitt (1) was the shocker. The West held few surprises but did produce one odd game: Michigan beat Tennessee without making a single free throw, an all-time tournament first! Back-to-back upsets by Marquette (11) in the East Region provided a little spark there, but all the other top teams advanced.

Sweet Sixteen and Elite Eight

VCU continued its amazing march, swamping Purdue and then nipping Florida State in overtime to reach the Elite Eight. They knocked off Kansas, picked by many—including **President Barack Obama**—as a possible champ, by 10 points. Out of nowhere, VCU was into the Final Four. Butler, meanwhile, continued its own upset march, beating Wisconsin easily. They needed overtime to beat Florida, but with the win completed an amazing return run to the Final Four.

UConn faced a tough San Diego State team and won, then squeaked out a two-point win over Arizona to reach the last dance.

In the East, the final game was a return to order, as a pair of basketball powerhouses tried to punch their Final Four tickets. Kentucky beat North Carolina and completed the Final Four (though the Wildcats did upset No. 1 Ohio State to get to their regional final clash).

Final Four

The VCU-Butler game was guaranteed to send a surprise team to the final game. VCU hung tough, but Butler's big-game experience paid off. VCU didn't shoot well, and Butler won by 10 points. In the other semifinal, UConn held off Kentucky in another defensive struggle. The Huskies' great last-minute free-throw shooting held on to the final one-point edge.

Championship Game

Butler went as cold as ice, shooting an all-time low 18.8 percent from the field. UConn took full advantage and closed out its third title in 11 years, winning, 53–41.

WHITE HOUSE BRACKET

President Obama filled out his NCAA tournament bracket and picked all four No. 1 seeds to make the Final Four. Like all but a tiny handful of people—from experts to everyday fans—he was wrong. He did pretty well in the first rounds, getting 29 of the first 32 games right. But then upsets by teams like Florida State, Butler, and VCU wrecked his (and lots of other people's) brackets. Plus, the president missed all the Final Four teams in the women's bracket, too!

IN THE PAINT

Upset . . . Not So Much

The first big upset of the season was a sign of things to come. In November, Connecticut faced off against Big Ten power Michigan State. UConn was unranked, while the Wolverines were the No. 2 team in the country, but the Huskies won, 70–67. Shades of things to come for UConn.

A Long Streak Ends

College basketball teams love to play at home. The cheering crowd and familiar court make winning easier. The Kansas Jayhawks had won 69 straight games at Rupp Arena, dating back to 2007, the longest such streak in the nation. But on January 22, though Kansas led Texas by as many as 15 points, Texas didn't quit. The Longhorns hung on to snap the streak, with a final score of 74–63.

The same weekend, another streak ended, along with one team's shot at No. 1. Unranked Notre Dame knocked off No. 2-ranked Pittsburgh at the Panthers' home court. It was the first time in 20 home games that Pitt had lost and knocked them out of the national top 5.

A Longer Streak Ends

Caltech entered its game against Occidental on February 22 riding a 310-game losing streak in its conference. It hadn't won a conference game in 26 years!

That all changed in February. With a 46–45 win over Occidental, Caltech ended the longest losing streak in NCAA sports history. Caltech's fans stormed the court to celebrate.

A LOOK AHEAD

If you'd picked UConn to come out on top this year, you'd have been the only one outside Connecticut to do so! But we'll check out our crystal basketball and peer ahead in the future. The 2012 men's NCAA basketball champion will be:

TOP PLAYER

Jimmermania hit BYU this season as the hot-shooting guard lit up scoreboards and set records. **Jimmer Fredette** led the nation with a 28.5 points-per-game average. He set a school record with 2,599 career points. He had 15 games with 30 or more points, including 4 with 40 or more. Though his BYU team fell in the Sweet Sixteen, it was a remarkable senior season. He won the Wooden and Naismith Awards as the top player in the nation. He was also named the AP Player of the Year.

Gimme a T!

Cheerleaders are supposed to help their teams win. A Louisville cheerleader almost did the opposite, however. In a February game against Pittsburgh, Louisville dunked to take a five-point lead. A male cheerleader sitting under the basket thought the game was over, and he grabbed the ball and threw it in the air in celebration. One problem: 0.5 second remained on the clock. The game was still on.

A referee gave Louisville a technical foul for the cheerleader's actions. Pitt made both of the free throws. Louisville then had a chance for a desperation shot to tie the game. The shot missed, and the Cardinals' cheerleader breathed a huge sigh of relief!

◂◂◂ Koach K's Konnection

Duke coach **Mike Krzyzewski** (it's pronounced "shu-SHEFS-skee" . . . trust us) reached a big milestone with Duke's NCAA tournament win over Michigan. It was his 900th victory as a head coach. (He's also tied with Adolph Rupp for the second-most NCAA titles with 4.) By the time you read this, Coach K will probably have won at least three more games. That would give him a new all-time NCAA Division I record, topping the old mark set by Bobby Knight.

WOMEN'S COLLEGE HOOPS

Stanford celebrates after snapping the streak.

Women's college basketball has been dominated by three schools for several seasons. Connecticut had won the previous two national titles, while going undefeated. Stanford and Tennessee were also regulars in the women's Final Four. However, when the dust settled after the 2010–11 season, a new champion had been crowned.

UConn came into the season aiming to top the record of 88 straight wins set by the UCLA men's team in the early 1970s. In an early-season showdown with up-and-coming Baylor (led by the amazing **Brittney Griner**, a 6'8" All-American), UConn kept the streak alive. UConn superstar **Maya Moore** scored 30 points, and UConn held on to win.

A couple of weeks later, though, the streak was over, after 90 straight wins. Stanford beat UConn, 71–59. Amazingly, Stanford was the last team to beat UConn, way back in 2008. UConn had been so dominant during its streak that it won every game but one by 10 points or more!

Baylor, UConn, and Stanford remained atop the rankings. UConn didn't lose, starting a new streak that it carried into its fourth straight Final Four appearance.

Once the NCAA tournament began, a pair of new teams started making noise with big wins. Notre Dame made it to the

FINAL TOP 10

ESPN/*USA Today*

1. Texas A&M
2. Notre Dame
3. Connecticut
4. Stanford
5. Baylor
6. Tennessee
7. Duke
8. Gonzaga
9. Green Bay
10. DePaul

Adams and Diggins faced off in an unlikely NCAA final.

Final Four, thanks to the outstanding play of **Skylar Diggins**. Then came the big shocker: UConn lost again! Notre Dame, led by Diggins's 28 points, shocked the Huskies in the semifinal and won, 72–63, to earn a spot in the championship game. It was the first loss by UConn in the national tournament since 2008.

The other national finalist was Texas A&M, making its first-ever appearance in the title game. To get there, it had to get through a tough Stanford team, the same team that had ended the UConn streak earlier in the season. But the women from Texas were not going to be upset, and they hung on to win an exciting semifinal game, 63–62.

As in the men's tournament, lower seeds took the main stage in the finals. It was the first women's championship without a No. 1 seed since 1994. In the final game, Texas A&M won its first national title in the sport, holding Diggins in check and beating Notre Dame, 76–70. **Danielle Adams** poured in 30 points for the Aggies and was named the Most Outstanding Player.

MAYA MOORE

Moore, a four-time All-American, ended her career as the UConn Huskies' career scoring leader, with 3,036 points, and ranked second in three-pointers and rebounds. Moore averaged 22.8 points, 8.2 rebounds, 2.3 steals, and 4.0 assists in the 2010–11 season.

She led UConn to four consecutive Final Fours and two national titles (2009 and 2010), as well as throughout their record-setting 90-game winning streak that spanned three seasons. She became only the third woman named player of the year twice.

NCAA CHAMPS

MEN'S DIVISION I

Brian Zoubek of 2010 champ Duke cuts down the net.

2011	**Connecticut**
2010	**Duke**
2009	**North Carolina**
2008	**Kansas**
2007	**Florida**
2006	**Florida**
2005	**North Carolina**
2004	**Connecticut**
2003	**Syracuse**
2002	**Maryland**
2001	**Duke**
2000	**Michigan State**
1999	**Connecticut**
1998	**Kentucky**
1997	**Arizona**
1996	**Kentucky**
1995	**UCLA**
1994	**Arkansas**
1993	**North Carolina**
1992	**Duke**
1991	**Duke**
1990	**UNLV**
1989	**Michigan**
1988	**Kansas**
1987	**Indiana**
1986	**Louisville**
1985	**Villanova**
1984	**Georgetown**
1983	**NC State**
1982	**North Carolina**
1981	**Indiana**
1980	**Louisville**
1979	**Michigan State**
1978	**Kentucky**
1977	**Marquette**
1976	**Indiana**
1975	**UCLA**
1974	**NC State**

1973 **UCLA**
1972 **UCLA**
1971 **UCLA**
1970 **UCLA**
1969 **UCLA**
1968 **UCLA**
1967 **UCLA**
1966 **Texas Western**
1965 **UCLA**
1964 **UCLA**
1963 **Loyola (Illinois)**
1962 **Cincinnati**
1961 **Cincinnati**
1960 **Ohio State**
1959 **California**
1958 **Kentucky**
1957 **North Carolina**
1956 **San Francisco**
1955 **San Francisco**
1954 **La Salle**
1953 **Indiana**
1952 **Kansas**
1951 **Kentucky**
1950 **City Coll. of N.Y.**
1949 **Kentucky**
1948 **Kentucky**
1947 **Holy Cross**
1946 **Oklahoma A&M**
1945 **Oklahoma A&M**
1944 **Utah**
1943 **Wyoming**
1942 **Stanford**
1941 **Wisconsin**
1940 **Indiana**
1939 **Oregon**

WOMEN'S DIVISION I

2011 **Texas A&M**
2010 **Connecticut**
2009 **Connecticut**
2008 **Tennessee**
2007 **Tennessee**
2006 **Maryland**
2005 **Baylor**
2004 **Connecticut**
2003 **Connecticut**
2002 **Connecticut**
2001 **Notre Dame**
2000 **Connecticut**
1999 **Purdue**
1998 **Tennessee**
1997 **Tennessee**
1996 **Tennessee**
1995 **Connecticut**
1994 **North Carolina**
1993 **Texas Tech**
1992 **Stanford**
1991 **Tennessee**
1990 **Stanford**
1989 **Tennessee**
1988 **Louisiana Tech**
1987 **Tennessee**
1986 **Texas**
1985 **Old Dominion**
1984 **USC**
1983 **USC**
1982 **Louisiana Tech**

UP, UP, AND AWAY!
Yes, that's a car. And yes, that's the Clippers' amazing dunking sensation Blake Griffin leaping over the car to make a slam. Griffin won the 2011 NBA Slam Dunk Contest with this auto- and gravity-defying flight.

NBA

DALLAS DOMINATES!

Heroes and villains. Sports is filled with heroes and villains. Sometimes, they're the same person. In the NBA, **LeBron James** has filled both roles, never more so than in 2010–11. Before that season, James announced "the Decision," and left the Cleveland Cavaliers for the Miami Heat. There, he joined two other superstars, **Dwyane Wade** and **Chris Bosh**. Heat fans loved it, packing the arena and cheering on the Big Three. Cavaliers fans hoped that James and his new team would fall on their faces.

Trophy time for Dallas owner Mark Cuban!

As the season moved along, the Heat had their ups and downs. The trio of stars had to learn to work together to share all the shots and points. But in the second half of the year, they meshed beautifully. The Big Three racked up the points, and the Heat looked nearly unbeatable. Who could challenge such a lineup of stars?

The defending-champion L.A. Lakers had a shot, most fans thought. The one-two punch of star guard **Kobe Bryant** and forward **Pau Gasol**, and the experience of coach **Phil Jackson**, made the Lakers the team to beat. But injuries slowed the Lakers down, and they stumbled in the play-offs. The Celtics were another threat to the Heat's rise, beating them in several key regular-season games. However, come play-off time, Miami's scoring machines were too tough for Boston to stop.

Miami's big three: Wade, Bosh, and James.

After the play-off dust settled (see page 86), one team stood between Miami and history: the Dallas Mavericks. Dallas had sort of flown under the radar in the regular season. They boasted a veteran team led by German superstar **Dirk Nowitzki** and 38-year-old guard **Jason Kidd**.

Not flashy or famous or exciting (Dallas owner **Mark**

Cuban usually got more attention than the players), Dallas nevertheless swept the Lakers and then beat up-and-coming Oklahoma City to capture a spot in the NBA Finals.

With their six-game victory (see page 87), the Mavericks put an end to the Heat's rise. At one point during the Finals, it seemed as if 49.5 states were rooting against Miami. (The other 0.5? South Florida!)

The title also pushed Nowitzki farther up the list of all-time greats. As an NBA star born in Germany, he was rare enough, but as a big man with a great outside shooting touch, he was rarer still. And now Nowitzki is more than a champion . . . he's the hero.

BIG MOVE

In 2010, the big move was James to the Heat. In 2011, the biggest move came when star guard **Carmelo Anthony** moved from the Denver Nuggets to the New York Knicks. Teaming with star center **Amar'e Stoudemire**, Anthony energized the Knicks. They finished second in the Atlantic Division and made the play-offs. They were swept there by Boston, but a full season of Anthony in 2011–12 might make the difference to an emerging Knicks team.

2010–11 FINAL STANDINGS

EASTERN CONFERENCE

ATLANTIC DIVISION	W	L
Boston	56	26
New York	42	40
Philadelphia	41	41
New Jersey	24	58
Toronto	22	60

CENTRAL DIVISION	W	L
Chicago	62	20
Indiana	37	45
Milwaukee	35	47
Detroit	30	52
Cleveland	19	63

SOUTHEAST DIVISION	W	L
Miami	58	24
Orlando	52	30
Atlanta	44	38
Charlotte	34	48
Washington	23	59

WESTERN CONFERENCE

NORTHWEST DIVISION	W	L
Oklahoma City	55	27
Denver	50	32
Portland	48	34
Utah	39	43
Minnesota	17	65

PACIFIC DIVISION	W	L
L.A. Lakers	57	25
Phoenix	40	42
Golden State	36	46
L.A. Clippers	32	50
Sacramento	24	58

SOUTHWEST DIVISION	W	L
San Antonio	61	21
Dallas	57	25
New Orleans	46	36
Memphis	46	36
Houston	43	39

2011 PLAY-OFFS

The NBA play-offs are a thrill fest of action, a merry-go-round of hoops hysteria, a magic show of moves and grooves . . . but enough jokes—here are some highlights!

SWEEP! The defending-champ Lakers fell to Dallas in four straight games. It was the first time the Lakers were swept out of the play-offs since 1999. ▶▶▶

RISE OF ROSE Chicago's **Derrick Rose** had already won the NBA MVP (page 88), but he "rose" even higher in the play-offs. He carried the Bulls back to the conference finals for the first time since the **Michael Jordan** days in the 1990s.

◀◀◀ **UPSET CITY** The Memphis Grizzlies pulled the biggest surprise of the entire postseason. They came in as the No. 8 seed in the West, but knocked off the No. 1 San Antonio Spurs. **Zach Randolph** of Memphis came up big in his battle with superstar **Tim Duncan**.

THUNDER ROLLS The Thunder was rumbling in the play-offs. Led by scoring champ **Kevin Durant**, the Oklahoma City Thunder earned a thrilling series win over Memphis. That gave them their first trip to the NBA conference finals.

PLAY-OFF RESULTS
(games won in parentheses)

FIRST ROUND

EASTERN CONFERENCE

Chicago OVER **Indiana (4-1)**
Miami OVER **Philadelphia (4-0)**
Boston OVER **New York (4-0)**
Atlanta OVER **Orlando (4-2)**

WESTERN CONFERENCE

Memphis OVER **San Antonio (4-2)**
L.A. Lakers OVER **New Orleans (4-2)**
Dallas OVER **Portland (4-2)**
Oklahoma City OVER **Denver (4-1)**

CONFERENCE SEMIFINALS

EASTERN CONFERENCE

Miami OVER **Boston (4-1)**
Chicago OVER **Atlanta (4-2)**

WESTERN CONFERENCE

Dallas OVER **L.A. Lakers (4-0)**
Oklahoma City OVER **Memphis (4-3)**

CONFERENCE FINALS

EASTERN CONFERENCE

Miami OVER **Chicago (4-1)**

WESTERN CONFERENCE

Dallas OVER **Oklahoma City (4-1)**

NBA FINALS

Dallas OVER **Miami (4-2)**

Nowitzki was the NBA Finals MVP.

NBA FINALS

GAME 1: Miami 92, Dallas 84
The Heat held Dallas to its lowest point total of the play-offs.

GAME 2: Dallas 95, Miami 93
Dirk Nowitzki led a 15-point fourth-quarter rally!

GAME 3: Miami 88, Dallas 86
A late **Chris Bosh** basket helped the Heat hold off the charging Mavs.

GAME 4: Dallas 86, Miami 83
Battling a fever, Nowitzki scored 10 points in the fourth quarter. James scored just 8 points in the game.

GAME 5: Dallas 112, Miami 103
Dallas won with another big fourth-quarter run.

GAME 6: Dallas 105, Miami 93
Nowitzki came up big again, as did **Jason Terry**, and Dallas won its first NBA championship.

SUPERSTARS!

ROSE RISES

The NBA is packed with young stars, players who seem just a couple of days out of high school. But the MVP award usually goes to a more established star. In 2011, however, one young player was so successful, he just had to get the big honor. At 22 years old, Chicago guard **Derrick Rose** became the youngest NBA MVP ever. Rose averaged 25 points a game and led the Bulls to the best record in the NBA. His aggressive play and all-around talents should make him a star for years to come.

TROPHIES!

MOST VALUABLE PLAYER	**Derrick Rose,** Chicago
DEFENSIVE PLAYER OF THE YEAR	**Dwight Howard,** Orlando
ROOKIE OF THE YEAR	**Blake Griffin,** L.A. Clippers
MOST IMPROVED PLAYER	**Kevin Love,** Minnesota
SIXTH MAN AWARD	**Lamar Odom,** L.A. Lakers
CITIZENSHIP AWARD	**Ron Artest,** L.A. Lakers
SPORTSMANSHIP AWARD	**Stephen Curry,** Golden State
COACH OF THE YEAR	**Tom Thibodeau,** Chicago

All-NBA

FIRST TEAM	SECOND TEAM
LeBron James, F, MIAMI	**Pau Gasol,** F, L.A. LAKERS ▶▶▶
Kevin Durant, F, OKLAHOMA CITY	**Dirk Nowitzki,** F, DALLAS
Dwight Howard, C, ORLANDO	**Amar'e Stoudemire,** C, NEW YORK
Kobe Bryant, G, L.A. LAKERS	**Dwyane Wade,** G, MIAMI
Derrick Rose, G, CHICAGO	**Russell Westbrook,** G, OKLAHOMA CITY

STAT KINGS

Here are the top players in some key statistics for 2010–11:

CATEGORY	PLAYER, TEAM	MARK
SCORING	**Kevin DURANT,** OKLAHOMA CITY	**27.7** ▶
REBOUNDS	**Kevin LOVE,** MINNESOTA	**15.2**
ASSISTS	**Steve NASH,** PHOENIX	**11.4**
◀ STEALS	**Chris PAUL,** NEW ORLEANS	**2.35**
BLOCKS	**Andrew BOGUT,** MILWAUKEE	**2.58**
FG PCT.	**Nene HILARIO,** DENVER	**.615**
3-PT. FG PCT.	**Matt BONNER,** SAN ANTONIO	**.457**
FT PCT.	**Stephen CURRY,** GOLDEN STATE	**.934**

HARDWOOD HIGHLIGHTS

30-30 MAN

A triple-double happens when a player has double figures in three stat categories in one game. Double-doubles are pretty good, too. Minnesota big man **Kevin Love** ran off a string of 53 straight games with at least 10 points and 10 rebounds. He even had a 30-30 in November, with 31 points and 31 boards. It was the first 30-30 in 28 years!

Long-Distance Champ!

In February, **Ray Allen** of the Celtics became the all-time career leader in career three-pointers. He ended the season with 2,612, overtaking the old leader, **Reggie Miller**, who had 2,560.

Phabulous Phil

Lakers coach **Phil Jackson** retired after the season. With 12 championships, he won more than any other coach in a major U.S. pro sport. Here's the full list: (with Chicago Bulls) 1991, 1992, 1993, 1995, 1996, 1997, 1998; (with L.A. Lakers) 2000, 2001, 2002, 2009, 2010.

We'll Miss You, No Matter What We Called You!

The great **Shaquille O'Neal** called it a career after the 2011 season. With 28,596 points in 19 seasons, plus four NBA championships, he's a surefire Hall of Famer and one of the biggest personalities in NBA history. Here are just a few of his many colorful nicknames:

The Big Aristotle
Shaq-Fu
The Big Shamrock
The Diesel
The Big Cactus
Superman

Short Shots

* **LeBron-less:** In their first season without **LeBron James**, the Cleveland Cavaliers felt his loss. They set an NBA record with 26 straight losses, on their way to an NBA-high 63 losses for the season.

◀◀◀ * **All-Star of All-Stars:** Lakers guard **Kobe Bryant** became the second player ever to win four All-Star Game MVP awards. **Bob Pettit**, who played in the 1950s and 1960s, was the first.

* **Road Happy:** Miami played well on the road. In December and January, the Heat won 13 straight games away from home. It was the fourth-longest streak in NBA history.

* **Was the Basket Covered?:** On March 13, the Milwaukee Bucks set a team record they didn't want to set: fewest points in a game (56). Not surprisingly, they lost to the Celtics, who set their own record: fewest points allowed!

* **Jolly Good Show:** The Nets and Raptors played a pair of games in London in March. The contests were the first regular-season overseas games in NBA history. The Nets won both, including a triple-overtime thriller in the second game. ▶▶▶

* **Tune In, Fans:** The excitement of the NBA season drew big crowds . . . to the TV. The ratings for regular-season games were up as much as 30 percent over 2009–10. Ratings for the play-offs and finals jumped up as well.

SEATTLE STORMS!

Seattle lived up to its name and "stormed" through the league. Led by WNBA MVP and Finals MVP **Lauren Jackson**, the Storm didn't lose a game in the play-offs, sweeping Los Angeles and then Phoenix before whomping Atlanta in the Finals. It was Seattle's first title since 2004.

The WNBA had some changes in 2010. The Sacramento Monarchs played their last season in 2009; their players were spread to other teams in the league. Then, before the 2011 season, the Detroit Shock packed up and moved to Tulsa, Oklahoma.

Parker boasted dominant skills.

Looking ahead to 2011, the WNBA is happy to welcome back Sparks star **Candace Parker.** *Sports Illustrated* called the 25-year-old a "basketball superwoman." She was the 2008 Rookie of the Year and MVP for L.A. However, she missed time while pregnant (with daughter Lailaa) and then with a shoulder injury. Having this all-around star for a whole season makes the Sparks a team to watch around play-off time.

STAT STARS

Stat leaders in the 2010 WNBA season:

STAT	PLAYER, TEAM	MARK
SCORING	**Diana TAURASI,** PHOENIX	22.7
REBOUNDS	**Tina CHARLES,** CONNECTICUT	11.7 ▶
ASSISTS	**Ticha PENICHEIRO,** LOS ANGELES	6.9
STEALS	**Tamika CATCHINGS,** INDIANA	2.3
FG PCT.	**Candice DUPREE,** PHOENIX	.664
3-PT. FG PCT.	**Leilani MITCHELL,** NEW YORK	.486

FINAL STANDINGS

EASTERN CONFERENCE

	W	L
Indiana	22	12
Atlanta	18	16
Detroit	18	16
Washington	16	18
Chicago	16	18
Connecticut	16	18
New York	13	21

WESTERN CONFERENCE

	W	L
Phoenix	23	11
Seattle	20	14
Los Angeles	18	16
San Antonio	15	19
Minnesota	14	20
Sacramento	12	22

Watch Out for . . . MAYA MOORE!

Maya Moore led the University of Connecticut to one of the most dominant runs in college hoops history. With Moore as their leading scorer and rebounder, the Huskies won a pair of national championships and also put together a record 90-game unbeaten streak. Moore moves to the WNBA for the 2011 season, and she's sure to make waves there. She was the No. 1 overall draft pick by the Minnesota Lynx.

STAT STUFF

NBA CHAMPIONS

The twosome of Michael Jordan and Phil Jackson won six titles.

2010–11 **Dallas**
2009–10 **L.A. Lakers**
2008–09 **L.A. Lakers**
2007–08 **Boston**
2006–07 **San Antonio**
2005–06 **Miami**
2004–05 **San Antonio**
2003–04 **Detroit**
2002–03 **San Antonio**
2001–02 **L.A. Lakers**
2000–01 **L.A. Lakers**
1999–00 **L.A. Lakers**
1998–99 **San Antonio**
1997–98 **Chicago**
1996–97 **Chicago**
1995–96 **Chicago**
1994–95 **Houston**
1993–94 **Houston**
1992–93 **Chicago**
1991–92 **Chicago**
1990–91 **Chicago**
1989–90 **Detroit**
1988–89 **Detroit**
1987–88 **L.A. Lakers**
1986–87 **L.A. Lakers**
1985–86 **Boston**
1984–85 **L.A. Lakers**
1983–84 **Boston**
1982–83 **Philadelphia**
1981–82 **L.A. Lakers**
1980–81 **Boston**
1979–80 **L.A. Lakers**
1978–79 **Seattle**
1977–78 **Washington**
1976–77 **Portland**
1975–76 **Boston**
1974–75 **Golden State**
1973–74 **Boston**
1972–73 **New York**

1971–72 **L.A. Lakers**
1970–71 **Milwaukee**
1969–70 **New York**
1968–69 **Boston**
1967–68 **Boston**
1966–67 **Philadelphia**
1965–66 **Boston**
1964–65 **Boston**
1963–64 **Boston**
1962–63 **Boston**
1961–62 **Boston**
1960–61 **Boston**
1959–60 **Boston**
1958–59 **Boston**
1957–58 **St. Louis**
1956–57 **Boston**
1955–56 **Philadelphia**
1954–55 **Syracuse**
1953–54 **Minneapolis**
1952–53 **Minneapolis**
1951–52 **Minneapolis**
1950–51 **Rochester**
1949–50 **Minneapolis**
1948–49 **Minneapolis**
1947–48 **Baltimore**
1946–47 **Philadelphia**

WNBA CHAMPIONS

2010 **Seattle**
2009 **Phoenix**
2008 **Detroit**
2007 **Phoenix**
2006 **Detroit**
2005 **Sacramento**
2004 **Seattle**
2003 **Detroit**
2002 **Los Angeles**
2001 **Los Angeles**
2000 **Houston**
1999 **Houston**
1998 **Houston**
1997 **Houston**

The Mercury met President Barack Obama in 2009.

NHL

TIME TO CELEBRATE!
The Boston Bruins celebrate as Vancouver goalie Roberto Luongo skates away sadly. Patrice Bergeron (second from right) has just scored the third goal in Game 7 of the Stanley Cup finals. The Bruins went on to win the game, 4–0, and capture the cup!

Bs ARE THE BEST

When the Boston Bruins won their first Stanley Cup in 39 years, it ended an NHL season that was filled with record-setting performances, more outdoor hockey, and a change to the All-Star Game format (see page 103).

The 2010–11 NHL season opened with all eyes on the Stanley Cup champions, the Chicago Blackhawks. But these Blackhawks were much different from the squad that won the cup. Several of those top players either were traded away or left as free agents. The Blackhawks were not as strong as they had been the year before, and it took them until the last day of the regular season to clinch a play-off spot.

As in past seasons, the Western Conference was very tough, with the Vancouver Canucks—led by the powerhouse **Sedin** twins (**Daniel** and **Henrik**) and their outstanding goalie, **Roberto Luongo**—at the top. By the season's end, the Canucks had the best record in the league.

Daniel and Henrik Sedin were twin stars.

The Eastern Conference–leading Washington Capitals, led by superstar **Alexander Ovechkin**, had a roller-coaster ride of a season. They played terribly for most of the first half before coming alive and rising to the top of the conference. The race for No. 1 in the East was close, with

The Bruins played in Prague.

Hockey in Europe

For the fourth year in a row, the first puck of the NHL season was dropped in Europe. On October 7, 2010, the Carolina Hurricanes and Minnesota Wild faced off in Helsinki, Finland, and the next day, the Columbus Blue Jackets and San Jose Sharks went at it in Stockholm, Sweden. A day later, the Boston Bruins and Phoenix Coyotes battled in Prague, Czech Republic.

the Philadelphia Flyers and the Pittsburgh Penguins bearing down on the Capitals.

The Penguins' **Sidney Crosby** provided one of the biggest headlines of the season, but not in a way he wanted. The NHL has been very concerned about hits to the head. The league put in a new rule that seriously penalizes players who hit an opponent in the head. Crosby was one of several players who were injured that way last season. In a game in January, he was checked into the glass by Tampa Bay's **Victor Hedman**. As a result, Crosby missed the rest of the regular season and all of the play-offs. The Penguins really could have used their ace scorer and leader.

In the end, the powerful Canucks faced an upset winner in the East, the Boston Bruins. The Bs came out on top!

Ovechkin led the Caps to the best record in the East.

FINAL STANDINGS

EASTERN CONFERENCE	PTS
Washington **Capitals***	**107**
Philadelphia **Flyers***	**106**
Boston **Bruins***	**103**
Pittsburgh **Penguins**	**106**
Tampa Bay **Lightning**	**103**
Montreal **Canadiens**	**96**
Buffalo **Sabres**	**96**
New York **Rangers**	**93**
Carolina **Hurricanes**	**91**
Toronto **Maple Leafs**	**85**
New Jersey **Devils**	**81**
Atlanta **Thrashers**	**80**
Ottawa **Senators**	**74**
New York **Islanders**	**73**
Florida **Panthers**	**72**

WESTERN CONFERENCE	PTS
Vancouver **Canucks***	**117**
San Jose **Sharks***	**105**
Detroit **Red Wings***	**104**
Anaheim **Ducks**	**99**
Nashville **Predators**	**99**
Phoenix **Coyotes**	**99**
Los Angeles **Kings**	**98**
Chicago **Blackhawks**	**97**
Dallas **Stars**	**95**
Calgary **Flames**	**94**
St. Louis **Blues**	**87**
Minnesota **Wild**	**86**
Columbus **Blue Jackets**	**81**
Colorado **Avalanche**	**68**
Edmonton **Oilers**	**62**

* Division winners

STANLEY CUP PLAY-OFFS

When the Boston Bruins' 6-foot-9 captain **Zdeno Chara** lifted the Stanley Cup over his head, it probably set a record for the highest the Cup has ever been lifted! The Bruins' 4–0 Game 7 win over the Vancouver Canucks gave them their first Stanley Cup in 39 years.

The battle for the 2011 Stanley Cup had plenty of surprises. One of the most eagerly anticipated matchups was the opening-round duel between the defending-champion Chicago Blackhawks and the league-leading Vancouver Canucks. The Canucks won the first three games, but the Blackhawks battled back and won the next three games, forcing a Game 7 showdown in Vancouver. The Canucks won a thrilling game on an overtime goal by **Alexandre Burrows**.

Meanwhile, the Bruins barely survived their first-round matchup against their archrivals, the Montreal Canadiens. The Bruins had to win three games in overtime, including Game 7, to push their way into the next round.

Chara is one of the tallest players in the NHL; here he's also the happiest!

In the next round, led by great goaltending by **Tim Thomas**, the Bruins swept the Flyers in four straight games. The Flyers weren't the only top-ranked team to get bounced out of the play-offs. The Pittsburgh Penguins were knocked out in a hard-fought seven-game series with the Tampa Bay Lightning.

Eventually, it all came down to the Bruins versus the Canucks in the Stanley Cup finals. It was the Bruins' first trip to the finals since 1990 and the Canucks' first since 1994. In the first game in Boston, the Bruins' sensational young forward, **Nathan Horton**, was knocked out in the first period by the Canucks' **Aaron Rome**. Rome was kicked out of the game, and the Bruins were inspired. In the second period, they erupted for four goals, added four more in the third, and blasted the Canucks, 8–1.

With the home teams winning each of the first six games, the Stanley Cup championship was decided in Game 7 in Vancouver. Horton didn't return to play in the series, but he

Vancouver won a big Game 7 vs. Chicago.

did go with his teammates to Vancouver. He knew the home ice advantage had to be broken, so before Game 7, Horton spilled melted ice from the Bruins' home rink, TD Garden, onto the Vancouver ice.

The Bruins scored their first goal just five minutes into the game. It spelled the beginning of the end for the Canucks. The Bs scored three more, and Thomas turned aside all of the Canucks' 37 shots—and the Bruins were champions!

Toughing It Out

Hockey players are known for being tough, but Tampa Bay's **Steven Stamkos** took it to another level in the 2011 play-offs. Stamkos's nose was broken in a matchup against the Bruins. He missed only a few minutes of action before returning to the game wearing a face shield and bandages over his shattered beak.

PLAY-OFF RESULTS

(Games won in parentheses)

FIRST ROUND

EASTERN CONFERENCE

Washington OVER **New York (4-1)**

Philadelphia OVER **Buffalo (4-3)**

Boston OVER **Montreal (4-3)**

Tampa Bay OVER **Pittsburgh (4-3)**

WESTERN CONFERENCE

Vancouver OVER **Chicago (4-3)**

San Jose OVER **Los Angeles (4-2)**

Detroit OVER **Phoenix (4-0)**

Nashville OVER **Anaheim (4-2)**

CONFERENCE SEMIFINALS

EASTERN CONFERENCE

Tampa Bay OVER **Washington (4-0)**

Boston OVER **Philadelphia (4-0)**

WESTERN CONFERENCE

Vancouver OVER **Nashville (4-2)**

San Jose OVER **Detroit (4-3)**

CONFERENCE FINALS

EASTERN CONFERENCE

Boston OVER **Tampa Bay (4-3)**

WESTERN CONFERENCE

Vancouver OVER **San Jose (4-1)**

STANLEY CUP FINALS

Boston OVER **Vancouver (4-3)**

HOCKEY HIGHLIGHTS

Record-setting Goals ▶▶▶

Penalty-shot goals are pretty rare, but for the first time in NHL history, four penalty-shot goals were scored on the same night. On October 30, the Florida Panthers' **David Booth**, the New York Islanders' **Frans Nielsen**, the New York Rangers' **Ryan Callahan**, and the Washington Capitals' **David Steckel** all put the puck into the net on their penalty-shot attempts.

Auspicious Start

New York Rangers rookie forward **Derek Stepan** became the first Ranger and only the fourth player in history to score three goals (known as a hat trick) in his first NHL game. He put the puck into the net three times against the Buffalo Sabres on October 9, 2010, the Rangers' season-opening game.

◀◀◀ Like Great-grandfather, Grandfather, Father, and Son

Blake Geoffrion (far left) played 20 games with the Nashville Predators in 2010–11. Blake is the first fourth-generation NHL player. His father, grandfather, and great-grandfather all played in the NHL. His grandfather was **Bernie "Boom-Boom" Geoffrion** (near left), a legendary goal scorer for the Montreal Canadiens and New York Rangers, who claimed to have invented the slapshot. Blake's great-grandfather was **Howie Morenz**, one of the NHL's first superstars in the 1930s. Blake's the latest to join the family's icy business.

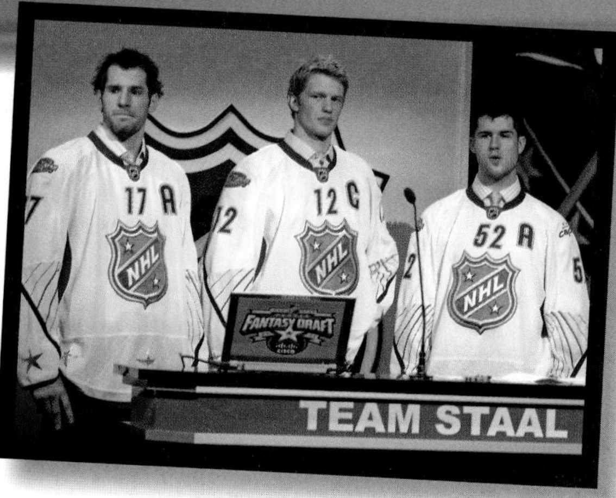

All-Star Game Chooses Up Sides ▸▸▸

It was like being on a playground . . . but with grown-ups. For the 2011 NHL All-Star Game, fans and coaches chose the players. But the two All-Star captains picked their own teams from those players. **Nicklas Lidstrom** and **Eric Staal** took turns choosing on live TV. Staal made sure to choose his brother **Marc**, saying his mother would never forgive him if he didn't! Team Lidstrom won the game, 11–10.

Outdoor Hockey

Fans wore raincoats rather than parkas when the annual Bridgestone Winter Classic was held outdoors at rainy Heinz Field in Pittsburgh on New Year's Day. Actually, it was New Year's Night—the game started at 8 P.M. due to the rain. The Penguins and Capitals skated through the drizzle as the Caps won the game, 3–1. In another outdoor game, the Flames beat the Canadiens, 4–0, in chilly Calgary, Canada.

COLLEGE HOCKEY

The Frozen Four

The NCAA Frozen Four is the championship of college hockey. North Dakota, Michigan, Notre Dame, and Minnesota Duluth made it there in 2011. The final game matched the Minnesota Duluth Bulldogs against the Michigan Wolverines. In overtime, **Kyle Schmidt**, playing in his final game at Minnesota Duluth, scored the game-winning goal to give his team its first NCAA championship.

Record-setting Crowd

A record crowd of 113,411 packed famed football palace Michigan Stadium to watch . . . a hockey game!

The Wolverines played their rivals, the Michigan State Spartans (above). Michigan won the game, 5-0. Their captain, **Carl Hagelin**, scored two goals in the win. The crowd shattered the previous ice-hockey record of 77,803, for a World Championship game in Germany earlier in 2010.

2010–11 AWARDS

Conn Smythe Trophy
(Stanley Cup Play-offs MVP)
TIM THOMAS, Boston Bruins

President's Trophy
(Best Regular-season Record: 117 points)
VANCOUVER CANUCKS

Hart Trophy (MVP)
COREY PERRY, Anaheim Ducks

Ted Lindsay Award
(Outstanding Player, as Voted by the Players)
DANIEL SEDIN, Vancouver Canucks

Vezina Trophy (Best Goaltender)
TIM THOMAS, Boston Bruins

James Norris Memorial Trophy
(Best Defenseman)
◀◀◀ **NICKLAS LIDSTROM,** Detroit Red Wings

Calder Memorial Trophy
(Best Rookie)
JEFF SKINNER, Carolina Hurricanes

Frank J. Selke Trophy
(Best Defensive Forward)
RYAN KESLER, Vancouver Canucks

Art Ross Trophy (Top Point Scorer)
DANIEL SEDIN, Vancouver Canucks

Maurice "Rocket" Richard Trophy
(Top Goal Scorer)
COREY PERRY, Anaheim Ducks

Lady Byng Memorial Trophy
(Most Gentlemanly Player)
MARTIN ST. LOUIS, Tampa Bay Lightning

Jack Adams Award (Best Coach)
DAN BYLSMA, Pittsburgh Penguins

What's Next? The NHL in 2011–12

HIT THE ROAD: The NHL will take its act to Europe again when Berlin, Helsinki, and Stockholm host games. The Anaheim Ducks, Buffalo Sabres, Los Angeles Kings, and New York Rangers will get their passports in order.

THE WINTER CLASSIC, ROUND FIVE: One of the NHL's great rivalries will take it outside when the Flyers host the New York Rangers at Citizens Bank Park for the Fifth Bridgestone Winter Classic.

PREDICTION: Who will come out ahead after all the off-season moves by teams? Which teams do we think will face off for the Cup? Look for a fast-paced showdown between the:

Los Angeles Kings AND Pittsburgh Penguins

In our crystal ball: Kings vs. Penguins in 2012.

THE OFF-SEASON

◎ **HERE COME THE JETS!** In 1995, the Jets left Winnipeg and moved to Phoenix to become the Coyotes. The fans in Canada were sad, but that ends this fall. A group of owners is moving the Atlanta Thrashers to Winnipeg and picking up the old Jets name. The area around Winnipeg is one of the most hockey-mad in Canada, so it will welcome the Jets with open arms.

◎ **FREE AGENCY** Two big stars will be on new teams in 2011–12. Center **Brad Richards** moves from the Dallas Stars to the New York Rangers. Also, NHL legend **Jaromir Jagr** is making a comeback. He played the past three years in Russia after a stellar career in Pittsburgh. But for his return to North America, he chose to sign with the Penguins' in-state rival—the Philadelphia Flyers. Will Penguins fans boo their hero when he visits?

◎ **THE TRADE SHUFFLE** The Philadelphia Flyers shook things up with two massive trades before the 2011–12 season. They acquired the rights to star goalie **Ilya Bryzgalov** but didn't have the money to sign him. So they traded center **Jeff Carter** to the Blue Jackets. Then they surprised everyone a few minutes later by trading their captain, **Mike Richards**, to the Kings for **Wayne Simmonds** and **Brayden Schenn**. And *then* they signed Bryzgalov.

STANLEY CUP CHAMPIONS

2010–11	**Boston Bruins**
2009–10	**Chicago Blackhawks**
2008–09	**Pittsburgh Penguins**
2007–08	**Detroit Red Wings**
2006–07	**Anaheim Ducks**
2005–06	**Carolina Hurricanes**
2004–05	No champion (Lockout)
2003–04	**Tampa Bay Lightning**
2002–03	**New Jersey Devils**
2001–02	**Detroit Red Wings**
2000–01	**Colorado Avalanche**
1999–00	**New Jersey Devils**
1998–99	**Dallas Stars**
1997–98	**Detroit Red Wings**
1996–97	**Detroit Red Wings**
1995–96	**Colorado Avalanche**
1994–95	**New Jersey Devils**
1993–94	**New York Rangers**
1992–93	**Montreal Canadiens**
1991–92	**Pittsburgh Penguins**
1990–91	**Pittsburgh Penguins**
1989–90	**Edmonton Oilers**
1988–89	**Calgary Flames**
1987–88	**Edmonton Oilers**
1986–87	**Edmonton Oilers**
1985–86	**Montreal Canadiens**
1984–85	**Edmonton Oilers**
1983–84	**Edmonton Oilers**
1982–83	**New York Islanders**
1981–82	**New York Islanders**
1980–81	**New York Islanders**
1979–80	**New York Islanders**
1978–79	**Montreal Canadiens**
1977–78	**Montreal Canadiens**
1976–77	**Montreal Canadiens**
1975–76	**Montreal Canadiens**
1974–75	**Philadelphia Flyers**
1973–74	**Philadelphia Flyers**
1972–73	**Montreal Canadiens**
1971–72	**Boston Bruins**
1970–71	**Montreal Canadiens**
1969–70	**Boston Bruins**
1968–69	**Montreal Canadiens**
1967–68	**Montreal Canadiens**
1966–67	**Toronto Maple Leafs**
1965–66	**Montreal Canadiens**
1964–65	**Montreal Canadiens**
1963–64	**Toronto Maple Leafs**
1962–63	**Toronto Maple Leafs**
1961–62	**Toronto Maple Leafs**
1960–61	**Chicago Blackhawks**
1959–60	**Montreal Canadiens**

1958–59	**Montreal Canadiens**
1957–58	**Montreal Canadiens**
1956–57	**Montreal Canadiens**
1955–56	**Montreal Canadiens**
1954–55	**Detroit Red Wings**
1953–54	**Detroit Red Wings**
1952–53	**Montreal Canadiens**
1951–52	**Detroit Red Wings**
1950–51	**Toronto Maple Leafs**
1949–50	**Detroit Red Wings**
1948–49	**Toronto Maple Leafs**
1947–48	**Toronto Maple Leafs**
1946–47	**Toronto Maple Leafs**
1945–46	**Montreal Canadiens**
1944–45	**Toronto Maple Leafs**
1943–44	**Montreal Canadiens**
1942–43	**Detroit Red Wings**
1941–42	**Toronto Maple Leafs**
1940–41	**Boston Bruins**
1939–40	**New York Rangers**
1938–39	**Boston Bruins**
1937–38	**Chicago Blackhawks**
1936–37	**Detroit Red Wings**
1935–36	**Detroit Red Wings**
1934–35	**Montreal Maroons**
1933–34	**Chicago Blackhawks**
1932–33	**New York Rangers**
1931–32	**Toronto Maple Leafs**
1930–31	**Montreal Canadiens**

The Anaheim Ducks won their only Cup in 2007.

1929–30	**Montreal Canadiens**
1928–29	**Boston Bruins**
1927–28	**New York Rangers**
1926–27	**Ottawa Senators**
1925–26	**Montreal Maroons**
1924–25	**Victoria Cougars**
1923–24	**Montreal Canadiens**
1922–23	**Ottawa Senators**
1921–22	**Toronto St. Pats**
1920–21	**Ottawa Senators**
1919–20	**Ottawa Senators**
1918–19	No decision
1917–18	**Toronto Arenas**

14
Office Depot
14
21
TREVOR BAYNE
21
Quick Lane
TIRE & AUTO CENTER
Motorcraft
Motorcraft
3M
Holley
MAHLE
JEGS

NASCAR

BUMPER-TO-BUMPER TRAFFIC
Drivers raced thisclose *at breakneck speeds around the 2.5-mile track at the historic Daytona 500 to kick off the 2011 Sprint Cup season in February. Twenty-year-old Trevor Bayne, in car 21, won and became the youngest winner in the history of the storied race.*

THE DRIVE TO FIVE!

Stop us if you've heard this one before: **Jimmie Johnson** won the Sprint Cup as NASCAR's season points champion for 2010. That's right, the same driver who won the championship in 2006, 2007, 2008, and 2009—no one else had ever won four titles in a row—won it all again for the record fifth year in a row. Ho-hum, right? Well, not exactly.

The result may have been the same, but getting there was a whole lot different. That's because, for the first time, Johnson had to come from behind to win. He entered the last race of the season trailing **Denny Hamlin** by 15 points. It was the closest that the top two drivers had been entering the last race since the Chase for the Cup began in 2004.

> ***"Jimmie Johnson just may be the best there's ever been. He has no weaknesses."***
>
> — NASCAR LEGEND **BOBBY ALLISON**

That was the kind of excitement NASCAR had in mind when it started the Chase. But all along in his record run, Johnson had things pretty much wrapped up going into the last race. All he usually had to do was make sure he didn't get into a big wreck, and he could coast to the championship.

Johnson outdueled Hamlin to win his fifth title . . . but it took him until the last race to clinch it.

Johnson can drive . . . and count!

MOST NASCAR SEASON POINTS TITLES

DRIVER	CHAMPIONSHIPS
Dale **Earnhardt Sr.**	**7**
Richard **Petty**	**7**
Jimmie **Johnson**	**5**
Jeff **Gordon**	**4**
David **Pearson**	**3**
Lee **Petty**	**3**
Darrell **Waltrip**	**3**
Cale **Yarborough**	**3**

By staying clear of accidents and finishing second in the race, Johnson won the season title by 39 points over Hamlin. Johnson thus became only the third NASCAR driver ever to win at least five championships in his career.

It was a terrific ending to one of the strangest NASCAR seasons ever. The season started with one of the most unusual sights you'll ever see on a racetrack: Officials had to fix a pothole at the famous Daytona 500! Later, many of the races leading up to the Chase were marred by altercations among drivers—on and off the track. Then, when the Chase began, **Clint Bowyer** roared to the front by winning the first race, only to be disqualified after a postrace inspection.

Things seemed to run more smoothly early in 2011. After **Trevor Bayne**'s big win at Daytona (see pages 108–109 and 115), the season started with 10 different winners in the first 15 races—and only one of those was Jimmie Johnson!

CHASE FOR THE CUP

2010 FINAL STANDINGS

DRIVER	POINTS
1. **Jimmie JOHNSON**	6,622
2. **Denny HAMLIN**	6,583
3. **Kevin HARVICK**	6,581
4. **Carl EDWARDS**	6,393
5. **Matt KENSETH**	6,294
6. **Greg BIFFLE**	6,247
7. **Tony STEWART**	6,221
8. **Kyle BUSCH**	6,182
9. **Jeff GORDON**	6,176
10. **Clint BOWYER**	6,155
11. **Kurt BUSCH**	6,142
12. **Jeff BURTON**	6,033

CHAMPIONSHIP CONTENDERS

At one point in the 2010 season, **Dale Earnhardt Jr.** called **Jimmie Johnson** the **Michael Jordan** of NASCAR. But not even Jordan led his NBA team to a championship every season. Is 2011 the year that someone finally steps up to knock Johnson out of Victory Lane? In alphabetical order, here are the drivers we think have the best chance to become the first NASCAR champion in a long time who is *not* named Jimmie Johnson.

Kyle Busch

Kyle's older brother, **Kurt Busch**, won the first Chase for the Cup in the 2004 season. Little brother has shown he can win even when his car is not the best in the field. His maturity as a driver means the family has a chance at another title.

Dale Earnhardt Jr.

He's the most popular driver in NASCAR. But he finished 21st in the season standings in 2010. A switch to the Hendrick Motorsports team put him in the same garage as Jimmie Johnson in 2011. Maybe Johnson's success has rubbed off, because "Little E" is a contender again.

Earnhardt's fans are desperate for him to win and carry on the tradition.

Carl Edwards

Edwards hinted about what was coming when he won the last two races of the 2010 season. He didn't exactly come out of nowhere, though. He's made the Chase every year except his rookie season in 2004. In 2008, he finished second only to Johnson.

Denny Hamlin

Hamlin got off to a slow start in the 2011 season after almost winning the

Carl Edwards celebrates with a backflip.

championship in 2010. But he won at Michigan International Speedway in June to get back in contention. Maybe Hamlin just peaked too soon in 2010 and is poised for a run at the title in 2011.

Kevin Harvick

The man they call Happy was anything but that after falling out of the Chase in 2009. He finished 19th overall that year. But he rebounded to finish 3rd in 2010 after placing in the top 10 in 26 of 36 races. Then he got off to a fast start in 2011. Maybe he'll be happy again!

Camping World Truck Series

Todd Bodine began racing in NASCAR's Sprint Cup series in 1992. (It was called the Winston Cup back then.) But he really found a home after he began racing in NASCAR's truck series in 2004. He won a couple of races on a limited schedule that year and was the season champ in 2006. In 2010, he won his second Camping World Truck Series title. He posted 17 top-five finishes in 25 events and won 4 times.

NATIONWIDE SERIES

After winning the Nationwide Series championship in 2009, **Kyle Busch** won 13 of the 29 Nationwide events he entered in 2010. But why shouldn't he? That's kind of like Major League Baseball's Boston Red Sox beating their AAA farm team in Pawtucket. (The Nationwide Series is NASCAR's "minor league." Its cars are a little lighter and a little less powerful than the Sprint Cup cars.)

Still, Busch didn't win the 2010 title, because he didn't race in 6 events on the schedule. **Brad Keselowski** was the champ after racing in all 35 events. He won 6 of them and finished in the top 10 in 29 of them. He won his first championship, after back-to-back third-place finishes in 2008 and 2009.

AROUND THE TRACK

And Baby Makes Three!

Jamie McMurray didn't make the Chase in 2010, but he did start the season by winning the Daytona 500. Then, in the summer, he won at the Indianapolis Motor Speedway in the Brickyard 400. Best of all? Jamie's wife, Christy, gave birth to a baby boy!

Busch's Triple

Kyle Busch pulled off an amazing triple play at the Bristol Motor Speedway in Tennessee in August 2010. By zooming to victory in all three of NASCAR's series—Camping World Truck, Nationwide, and Sprint–Busch became the first driver to win in all three series at the same track in the same week.

New for 2011: CHOOSE ONE!

Kyle Busch, **Carl Edwards**, **Brad Keselowski**, and others have raced for championships in more than one of the three national series in the same year. NASCAR calls that double-dipping. But no more. In 2011, the official drivers' applications had a new section: "A driver will only be permitted to earn driver championship points in one of the following three series: NASCAR Sprint Cup, NASCAR Nationwide, or NASCAR Camping World Truck Series. Please select the series in which you would like to accumulate driver championship points. Choose one."

Youth Is Served

NASCAR kicked off its 2011 season with one of the most exciting Daytona 500 races ever. The lead changed hands a record 74 times among 22 drivers, another record. **Trevor Bayne** was the last to lead and became, at just 20 years old, the youngest Daytona winner ever.

Will She or Won't She?

It just wouldn't be a NASCAR section without some mention of **Danica Patrick**. Once again, she's considering a jump from open-wheel cars to stock cars. The IndyCar racer went halfway in 2010 and had a rough go of it. She started 13 NASCAR races and never placed higher than 19th. At the Sam's Town 300 in March 2011, however, she was 4th. It was the highest finish ever by a woman in one of NASCAR's top three series. That, of course, led to reports—again—that Danica would make a full-time go of it in stock-car racing in 2012. We'll see!

2011 NASCAR CHAMPION

Halfway through the 2011 NASCAR season, the race for the championship was wide open. Five-time winner **Jimmie Johnson** was in the hunt, as usual. But so were **Kyle Busch**, **Jeff Gordon**, **Denny Hamlin**, and a bunch of other drivers. So is this the year that someone other than Johnson finally wins the title? Our book went to press too early to tell for sure, but we're going to go out on a limb and predict that NASCAR has a new champion for 2011. Our best guess for the 2011 Chase for the Cup champion is:

★Carl Edwards★

NASCAR CHAMPIONS

Year	Driver	Make
2010	Jimmie Johnson	Chevrolet
2009	Jimmie Johnson	Chevrolet
2008	Jimmie Johnson	Chevrolet
2007	Jimmie Johnson	Chevrolet
2006	Jimmie Johnson	Chevrolet
2005	Tony Stewart	Chevrolet
2004	Kurt Busch	Ford
2003	Matt Kenseth	Ford
2002	Tony Stewart	Pontiac
2001	Jeff Gordon	Chevrolet
2000	Bobby Labonte	Pontiac
1999	Dale Jarrett	Ford
1998	Jeff Gordon	Chevrolet
1997	Jeff Gordon	Chevrolet
1996	Terry Labonte	Chevrolet
1995	Jeff Gordon	Chevrolet
1994	Dale Earnhardt Sr.	Chevrolet
1993	Dale Earnhardt Sr.	Chevrolet
1992	Alan Kulwicki	Ford
1991	Dale Earnhardt Sr.	Chevrolet
1990	Dale Earnhardt Sr.	Chevrolet
1989	Rusty Wallace	Pontiac
1988	Bill Elliott	Ford
1987	Dale Earnhardt Sr.	Chevrolet
1986	Dale Earnhardt Sr.	Chevrolet
1985	Darrell Waltrip	Chevrolet
1984	Terry Labonte	Chevrolet
1983	Bobby Allison	Buick
1982	Darrell Waltrip	Buick
1981	Darrell Waltrip	Buick
1980	Dale Earnhardt Sr.	Chevrolet
1979	Richard Petty	Chevrolet
1978	Cale Yarborough	Oldsmobile
1977	Cale Yarborough	Chevrolet
1976	Cale Yarborough	Chevrolet
1975	Richard Petty	Dodge
1974	Richard Petty	Dodge
1973	Benny Parsons	Chevrolet

1972	Richard Petty	Plymouth
1971	Richard Petty	Plymouth
1970	Bobby Isaac	Dodge
1969	David Pearson	Ford
1968	David Pearson	Ford
1967	Richard Petty	Plymouth
1966	David Pearson	Dodge
1965	Ned Jarrett	Ford
1964	Richard Petty	Plymouth
1963	Joe Weatherly	Pontiac
1962	Joe Weatherly	Pontiac
1961	Ned Jarrett	Chevrolet
1960	Rex White	Chevrolet
1959	Lee Petty	Plymouth
1958	Lee Petty	Oldsmobile
1957	Buck Baker	Chevrolet
1956	Buck Baker	Chrysler
1955	Tim Flock	Chrysler
1954	Lee Petty	Chrysler
1953	Herb Thomas	Hudson
1952	Tim Flock	Hudson
1951	Herb Thomas	Hudson
1950	Bill Rexford	Oldsmobile
1949	Red Byron	Oldsmobile

NASCAR'S WINNINGEST DRIVERS

(career Cup series victories entering 2011)

DRIVER	RACES WON
1. Richard PETTY	200
2. David PEARSON	105
3. Bobby ALLISON	84
Darrell WALTRIP	84
5. Cale YARBOROUGH	83
6. Jeff GORDON	82
7. Dale EARNHARDT Sr.	76
8. Rusty WALLACE	55
9. Jimmie JOHNSON	54
Lee PETTY	54

OH, NO!
Rookie driver J. R. Hildebrand (at left) crashes into the wall on the last turn of the last lap of the 2011 Indianapolis 500. Hildebrand was leading the race at the time, but Dan Wheldon (bottom right) zoomed past him at the finish line to win. *(See page 122.)*

OTHER MOTOR SPORTS

FORMULA ONE

The Youngest Champ

Germany's **Sebastian Vettel** became the youngest Formula One season champ ever in 2010. Vettel was just 23 years old when he took the checkered flag at the Abu Dhabi Grand Prix in November. By winning that race, Vettel leapfrogged **Fernando Alonso** and **Mark Webber** into first place in the championship points race.

Vettel's victory put an exclamation point on the season. In addition to Vettel, Alonso, and Webber, defending champ **Jenson Button** and **Lewis Hamilton** made a run at the title. The lead changed nine times over the course of the 19-race schedule. Vettel never led . . . until the end.

"After crossing the line, my engineer came on the radio and said, 'It is looking good, but we have to wait until the other cars finish.' I was thinking, 'What does he mean?' Then he again came on and screamed at me that I had won the championship."

— **SEBASTIAN VETTEL**, ON HIS 2010 FORMULA ONE TITLE

2010 F1 FINAL STANDINGS

PLACE/DRIVER	POINTS
1. Sebastian Vettel	256
2. Fernando Alonso	252
3. Mark Webber	242
4. Lewis Hamilton	240
5. Jenson Button	214

Big Mistake

How seriously do they take Formula One racing in Europe? Well, one official in the Italian government called on the chairman of Ferrari—not the leader of the racing team, but of the whole company!—to resign after Spain's Alonso failed to win the championship in 2010. (The chairman didn't.)

Here's what happened: Alonso, who drives a Ferrari, entered the last race at Abu Dhabi in first place. The 2005 and 2006 champ, he needed only to finish in fourth place or better to guarantee the title, no matter what the other drivers did. Alonso qualified in third place and was in a good position most of the race. Then his team made a key mistake in strategy late in the race: The team called him in for a pit stop. When Alonso got back on the track, he had fallen out of fourth place. He finished seventh in the race and second in the overall standings.

New for 2011

Two big changes had Formula One drivers and fans uncertain about how their teams would do in 2011. One was a new rear wing on the open-wheel cars. It replaced a wing on the front. At certain times in a race, the driver is allowed to adjust the wing. It reduces drag and increases speed, making passing easier. The other change: new tires. Pirelli replaced Bridgestone as the official tire supplier for Formula One.

Because of the changes, defending champ Vettel said he wasn't sure where he stood compared to other drivers entering 2011. "But we have a good feeling," he said. His feeling didn't lie: Vettel finished first or second in each of the first eight races and built up a huge lead in the overall standings.

Coming in 2012: Back in the U.S.A.!

Though there still was no American team in Formula One in 2011, fans in the United States have 2012 to look forward to. That year, a race in the U.S. is on the Formula One schedule for the first time since 2007. The site: Austin, Texas. That's where a new track, called the Circuit of the Americas, is being built. The lead investor for the track is **Red McCombs**, former owner of the NFL's Minnesota Vikings.

New rules and gear made passes like this one easier in 2011.

INDYCAR WRAP-UP

Classic Indy ▶

The famous Indianapolis 500 celebrated its 100th running in the spring of 2011. The classic race was, well, a classic! Veteran **Dan Wheldon** (right) won the race for the second time.

The driver everyone was talking about, however, was **J. R. Hildebrand**. The rookie was about to win the Indianapolis 500 in his first try, leading the field on the last lap. All Hildebrand had to do was make it to the finish line. But he tried to pass a car that was a lap behind. He drifted too far outside, lost control, and hit the wall. Wheldon passed him for the win.

◀ Dario Does It Again

In 2010, for the second season in a row, **Dario Franchitti** (left) entered the final race of the IndyCar season trailing the leader in the season standings. And for the second season in a row, Franchitti emerged from that race as the season champ.

Will Power led Franchitti by 12 points entering the 2010 finale in Miami. But Power finished in 25th place. Franchitti led for 128 of the 200 laps, and then only had to play it safe. He finished in eighth place in the race and beat Power for the title by five points.

Earlier in the year, Franchitti won the Indianapolis 500 for the second time. He thus became part of a group of only five elite racers with two Indy 500 wins and three IndyCar season championships.

Despite the disappointing finish in 2010, Power got off to a strong start in 2011, with three early-season wins. At the halfway point of the season, he was in second place overall—right behind Franchitti.

2010 IZOD INDYCAR SERIES FINAL STANDINGS

PLACE/DRIVER	POINTS
1. Dario Franchitti	602
2. Will Power	597
3. Scott Dixon	547
4. Helio Castroneves	531
5. Ryan Briscoe	482

DRAGSTERS!

AGELESS WONDERS

The National Hot Rod Association (NHRA) produced its oldest and youngest season champs in 2010. **John Force** was 61 when he won the Funny Car division; **Louis Tonglet** was the Pro Stock Motorcycle champ at 20. It was Force's 15th national title. Tonglet, meanwhile, was still a teenager when he began his rookie year in the NHRA.

Other NHRA champs in 2010 included **Larry Dixon** in Top Fuel and **Greg Anderson** in Pro Stock. Dixon was the first Top Fuel winner not named **Tony Schumacher** since . . . . Larry Dixon in 2003. Schumacher's run of six consecutive titles ended when he finished in second place. Anderson's championship was his fourth, but his first since 2005.

One for the old guys: Force won his 15th title.

2010 NHRA CHAMPS

PLACE/DRIVER	POINTS
TOP FUEL	
1. Larry Dixon	2,684
2. Tony Schumacher	2,582
3. Cory McClenathan	2,551
FUNNY CAR	
1. John Force	2,621
2. Matt Hagan	2,579
3. Ashley Force Hood	2,449
PRO STOCK	
1. Greg Anderson	2,591
2. Greg Stanfield	2,479
3. Mike Edwards	2,469
PRO STOCK MOTORCYCLE	
1. Louis Tonglet	2,681
2. Andrew Hines	2,677
3. Ed Krawiec	2,559

Tonglet was a rookie sensation on the bike.

MOTOCROSS

Reed, who won the title in 2004 and 2008, did all he could by winning the finale. But Villopoto's third-place finish earned him enough points to defeat Reed for the overall championship. Dungey finished third in the standings and Stewart was fourth.

Stewart was the leader early in the final event, but he crashed 6 laps into the 20-lap race. That was pretty much how his season went. Stewart won 5 of the 17 events on the schedule but wiped out in several races.

IT'S ALL GOOD FOR VILLOPOTO

After the 2011 schedule ended, the American Motorcyclist Association (AMA) called it "the greatest supercross season ever." It certainly was for **Ryan Villopoto**, who edged out **Chad Reed** in a dramatic finish to win the AMA supercross championship for the first time.

Villopoto and Reed went back and forth all season long, with defending champ **Ryan Dungey** and **James "Bubba" Stewart Jr.** also in the chase. Villopoto led Reed by just nine points entering the last race at Sam Boyd Stadium in Las Vegas, Nevada.

DUNGEY SWEEPS

Ryan Dungey completed a supercross/motocross sweep in 2010 when he won the Lucas Oil AMA Pro Motocross championship. Earlier in 2010, Dungey won the title in supercross, which ends in May, by winning 6 of 17 events. Then Dungey dominated in motocross, which runs from May to September. He won 19 of 24 races to finish way ahead of runner-up **Brett Metcalfe**.

On the women's side, **Jessica Patterson** dethroned 2009 champion **Ashley Fiolek** as the motocross champ. Patterson won the first 6 of 16 races and never finished lower than second place.

NEED FOR SPEED!

Driver **Bobby Cleveland** and his 104-octane racing team went to the famed Bonneville Salt Flats in Utah in pursuit of a new world land-speed record in September 2010. Cleveland and his mates whooped it up after setting the mark at 96.529 miles per hour. Oh, one thing: It was a world speed record for a lawn mower! That's right. It had to be an actual working lawn mower, too. So to make it all official, a member of Cleveland's team put down a patch of real grass on the barren desert terrain. Cleveland mowed the grass, and the record was in the books!

Cleveland wasn't the lawn mower Driver of the Year for 2010, though. That award, presented by the United States Lawn Mower Racing Association (USLMRA), went to Michigan's **Richard Webb**.

Speed mowing really cuts down chore time!

Foust drove the world's biggest Hot Wheels car.

Other daredevil drivers in 2010–11:

➔ In the spring of 2011, X Games Rally Car gold medalist **Tanner Foust** (above) was the secret "Yellow Driver" in a record-setting stunt for Hot Wheels before the Indianapolis 500. Engineers draped a 1,500-foot-long orange track over the top of a 100-foot-high "bedroom door." Foust raced down the track, up a ramp, and through the air on a world-record jump of 332 feet.

➔ In a stadium built on Lake Havasu for the event, thousands of fans watched the International Jet Sports Boating Association World Finals. **Jean Baptiste**, **Justin Farthing**, and **Lee Stone** each won their pro division personal watercraft races.

➔ On the snow, **P. J. Wanderscheid** won his record fourth World Championship Snowmobile Derby in 2011. The 48th annual event was held, as always, in the third week of January in Eagle River, Wisconsin.

POWERBOAT RACING

Finland's **Sami Seliö** won the F1H20 Powerboat World Championship in 2010. Seliö beat American **Jay Price** (who races for the Qatar team) by six points in the closest season championship race since 2000. It was Seliö's second world title, with the first coming in 2007.

The season-long F1 Powerboat series is a lot like auto racing's F1 series. But when powerboat racers zip across the water at speeds of up to 140 miles per hour and make hairpin turns, they generate g-forces more like a fighter jet's.

Seliö took control of his destiny in the points race when he edged Price to win the Grand Prix of the United Arab Emirates in the next-to-last race of the season, in December 2010 in Abu Dhabi. One week later, in Sharjah in the United Arab Emirates, the "Finnish Flyer" earned enough points to be the champ.

In 2011, while Seliö got off to a slow start defending his championship, Price won the first two races of the season and soared to the top of the standings.

CHANGING OF THE GUARD

Italy's **Guido Cappellini** was the dominant force in F1 powerboat racing for nearly 20 years before he retired in 2010. Cappellini was nicknamed "Crashalini" early in his career because he wrecked his boat so many times. But he soon got things figured out. He won 10 world championships in 17 seasons, beginning in 1993. The last of his titles came in 2009, and then he hung up his helmet.

ODDS AND ENDS

DRIFTING ▸▸▸

One of the fastest-growing motor sports around is drifting. It combines the driving skills of rally car racing with the showmanship of freestyle motocross. Drivers slide sideways through a series of turns at high speed. The winner is not necessarily the one who completes the course the fastest. Instead, judges award points for technique and style—including crowd reaction!

Since 2007, a pro series called Formula Drift (or Formula D for short) has crowned a champion in the United States. In 2010, **Vaughn Gittin Jr.** won his first title in his Monster Energy Ford Mustang.

DAKAR RALLY

The most famous rally race in the world is the Dakar Rally. The nearly 6,000-mile race was held in Argentina and Chile in January 2011. Some 407 teams began the competition in Argentina on motorcycles and ATVs and in cars and trucks. Only about half of the teams finished.

In the trucks division, Russia's **Vladimir Chagin** was the fastest. He won his seventh championship, the most by any driver in any category. Other winners in 2011 included Spain's **Marc Coma** in motorcycles, Argentina's **Alejandro Patronelli** in ATVs, and Qatar's **Nasser Al-Attiyah** and Germany's **Timo Gottschalk** in cars (co-drivers).

Monster Trucks

The Monster Truck Racing Association (MTRA) named **Mark Hall** of Raminator the Driver of the Year for 2010. Teammate **Mat Dishman** of Rammunition was the Rookie of the Year. TailGator (left) was the Truck of the Year. It was the third year in a row that the 9,800-pound behemoth earned at least a share of the Truck of the Year award.

MAJOR CHAMPIONS OF THE 2000s

TOP FUEL DRAGSTERS

YEAR	DRIVER
2010	Larry Dixon
2009	Tony Schumacher
2008	Tony Schumacher
2007	Tony Schumacher
2006	Tony Schumacher
2005	Tony Schumacher
2004	Tony Schumacher
2003	Larry Dixon
2002	Larry Dixon
2001	Kenny Bernstein
2000	Gary Scelzi

FUNNY CARS

YEAR	DRIVER
2010	John Force
2009	Robert Hight
2008	Cruz Pedregon
2007	Tony Pedregon
2006	John Force
2005	Gary Scelzi
2004	John Force
2003	Tony Pedregon
2002	John Force
2001	John Force
2000	John Force

PRO STOCK CARS

YEAR	DRIVER
2010	Greg Anderson
2009	Mike Edwards
2008	Jeg Coughlin Jr.
2007	Jeg Coughlin Jr.
2006	Jason Line
2005	Greg Anderson
2004	Greg Anderson
2003	Greg Anderson
2002	Jeg Coughlin Jr.
2001	Warren Johnson
2000	Jeg Coughlin Jr.

FORMULA ONE

YEAR	DRIVER
2010	Sebastian Vettel
2009	Jenson Button
2008	Lewis Hamilton
2007	Kimi Raikkonen
2006	Fernando Alonso
2005	Fernando Alonso
2004	Michael Schumacher
2003	Michael Schumacher
2002	Michael Schumacher
2001	Michael Schumacher
2000	Michael Schumacher

INDYCAR SERIES

YEAR	DRIVER
2010	Dario Franchitti
2009	Dario Franchitti
2008	Scott Dixon
2007	Dario Franchitti
2006	Sam Hornish Jr. and Dan Wheldon (tie)
2005	Dan Wheldon
2004	Tony Kanaan
2003	Scott Dixon
2002	Sam Hornish Jr.
2001	Sam Hornish Jr.
2000	Buddy Lazier

AMA SUPERCROSS

YEAR	DRIVER
2011	Ryan Villopoto
2010	Ryan Dungey
2009	James Stewart Jr.
2008	Chad Reed
2007	James Stewart Jr.
2006	Ricky Carmichael
2005	Ricky Carmichael
2004	Chad Reed
2003	Ricky Carmichael
2002	Ricky Carmichael
2001	Ricky Carmichael
2000	Jeremy McGrath

AMA MOTOCROSS

YEAR	RIDER (MOTOCROSS)	RIDER (LITES)
2010	Ryan Dungey	Trey Canard
2009	Chad Reed	Ryan Dungey
2008	James Stewart Jr.	Ryan Villopoto
2007	Grant Langston	Ryan Villopoto
2006	Ricky Carmichael	Ryan Villopoto
2005	Ricky Carmichael	Ivan Tedesco
2004	Ricky Carmichael	James Stewart Jr.
2003	Ricky Carmichael	Grant Langston
2002	Ricky Carmichael	James Stewart Jr.
2001	Ricky Carmichael	Mike Brown
2000	Ricky Carmichael	Travis Pastrana

Ricky Carmichael

ACTION SPORTS

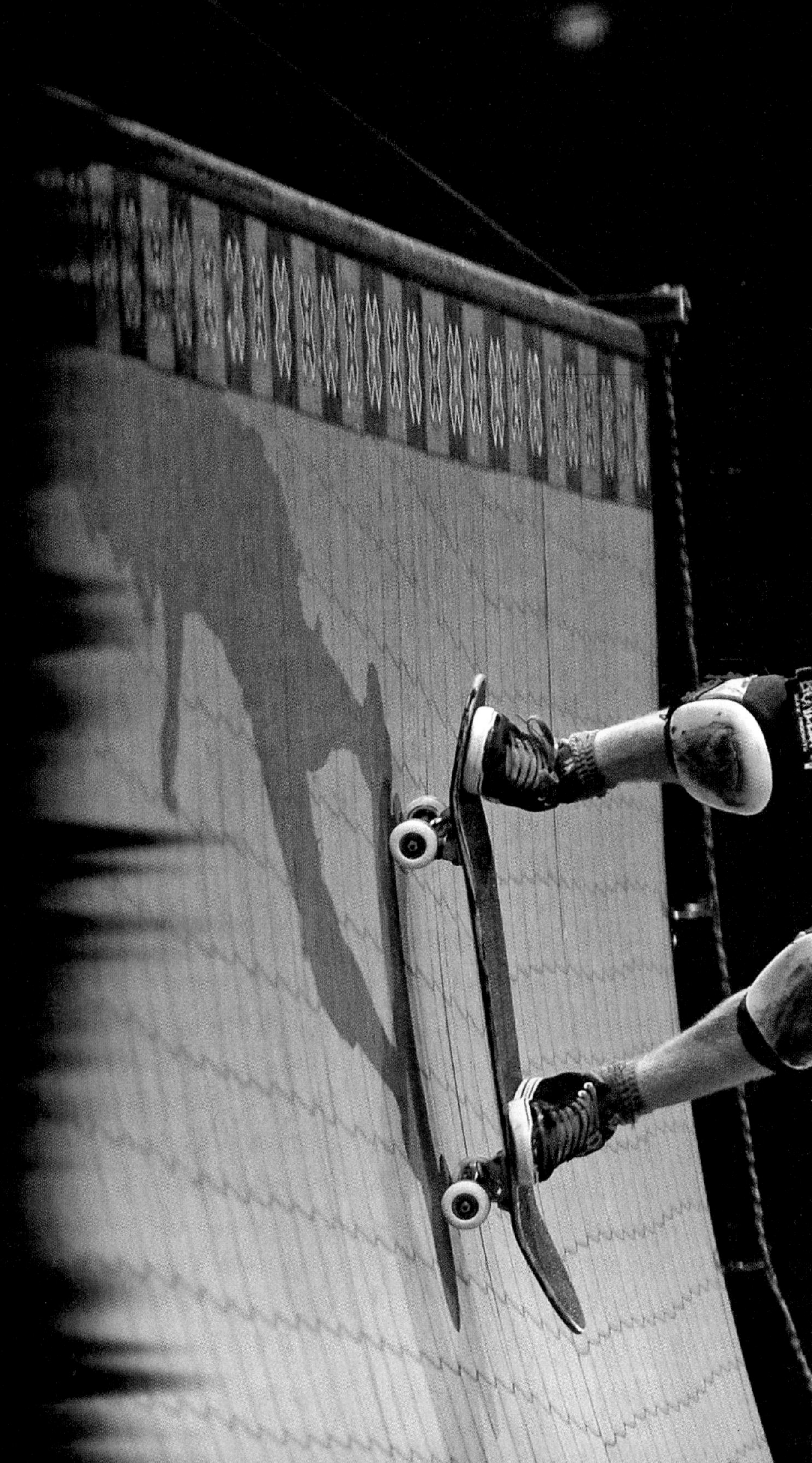

MAN FOR ALL SEASONS

Six months after winning his fourth consecutive gold medal in the snowboard superpipe at Winter X Games 15 in Aspen, Colorado, Shaun White took home a gold in Summer X Games 17 in Los Angeles. The action sports superstar upended three-time defending champ Pierre-Luc Gagnon in the skate vert competition. *(See page 137.)*

2010-2011 WRAP-UP

No doubt about it: Kelly Slater is the best surfer in the world.

Slater Hangs Ten

Legendary surfer **Kelly Slater** won the Association of Surfing Professionals (ASP) men's world championship for a record 10th time in 2010. And like a big wave that starts out in the ocean and gradually swells in size and strength, one question soon began gaining momentum: Is Slater the greatest athlete ever? (We're talking *any* sport here, not just surfing!)

The question was first posed by former *Surfer Magazine* editor **Chris Mauro** on GrindTV.com. It was picked up from there by **Dan Patrick** on his nationwide radio show. Then even the *New York Times* got in on it.

The final opinion? Slater says it's silly to compare athletes from different sports when you can't even compare athletes from different eras in the same sport. "If you can't go head-to-head in something, you can't prove anything," he told the *New York Times*. Still, Slater is in the discussion—which means surfing has come a long way.

> ***"I wasn't getting on Dan Patrick's show after nine [championships]. I had to get to ten."***
>
> — **KELLY SLATER**, AS QUOTED IN THE *NEW YORK TIMES*

Remembering Andy Irons

Slater's championship celebration at an event in Puerto Rico in November 2010 was muted by the death of three-time world champ **Andy Irons** (left) a few days earlier. The 32-year-old Irons had pulled out of the Puerto Rico event because of illness. He was on his way home to Hawaii when he had a heart attack during a stop in Texas.

Carissa Moore (left) and Stephanie Gilmore

Skiers Soar

The Canadian team dominated the International Ski Federation's Freestyle World Ski Championships at the Deer Valley Resort and the Park City Mountain Resort, Utah, in 2011. Canadian skiers took home gold medals in 8 of the 12 events. **Jennifer Heil** won multiple golds, winning the moguls and dual moguls.

The host Americans won seven medals. Their lone gold medal was earned by **Alex Schlopy** in the slopestyle.

Surfer Girls

After emerging as a major threat in her first season in 2010, American **Carissa Moore** ended Australian **Stephanie Gilmore**'s reign atop women's surfing in 2011.

Gilmore won the ASP women's world title for the fourth consecutive year in 2010. She won four of the eight events on tour and easily outdistanced fellow Aussie **Sally Fitzgibbons**, who was the runner-up. Moore, who was just 17 when she made her debut on tour, finished third.

Moore, however, was the surfer to beat in 2011. The Hawaiian won three of the first five stops on the schedule and became the youngest ASP world champ.

Grete Eliassen can really get off the ground.

Norway's **Grete Eliassen**, a former X Games medalist, didn't earn a medal in Utah. But she made news in 2010 with a record big air jump off a ramp in Utah. She soared 31 feet off the ground. It was the highest ever by a female skier. Eliassen had to reach a speed of 60 miles per hour to make her jump.

WINTER DEW TOUR 2010–11

CHAMPION	EVENT
Kevin Rolland*	Freeski Superpipe
Bobby Brown	Freeski Slopestyle
Louie Vito	Snowboard Superpipe
Kelly Clark	Women's Snowboard Superpipe
Torstein Horgmo*	Snowboard Slopestyle
Jamie Anderson*	Women's Snowboard Slopestyle

* Winter Dew Tour Athlete of the Year

Nitro Circus—Live!

Travis Pastrana's Nitro Circus went live in 2011. *Nitro Circus* debuted on Fuel TV in 2006 and later ran on MTV. It featured Pastrana and his friends doing what they do—racing bikes and performing stunts. Nitro Circus Live is Nitro Circus, well, live! Pastrana assembled a star-studded cast of action sports stars, including **Bob Burnquist**, **Cam Sinclair**, **Chad Kagy**, **Levi Sherwood**, **Jake Brown**, **Lyn-Z Adams Hawkins**, and more. They ride their bikes and boards and do their stunts in front of a live audience.

Nitro Circus Live debuted at the MGM Grand in Las Vegas in June 2011. The highlight of the show was a synchronized double backflip by Pastrana and Sinclair.

Travis Pastrana knows how to put on a show.

Skateboarder Lyn-Z Adams Hawkins was sky-high after a surprise marriage proposal.

Only a couple of years earlier, Sinclair was nearly killed when he crashed while trying to perform a double backflip. This time, the two superstars pulled it off side by side, and the crowd roared.

The double double backflip was the highlight of the show for the audience. But Pastrana and Adams Hawkins, a top pro skateboarder, might remember something else, too. Before the theatrics began, Pastrana dropped to one knee and surprised Adams Hawkins by asking her to marry him. She said yes.

Crash Landing

There were lots of other memorable action-sports stunts from Nitro Circus Live in Las Vegas, including an amazing big-air

> ***"I wasn't supposed to do this until the end of the show, but I was so nervous I couldn't wait."***
>
> — **TRAVIS PASTRANA**, WHILE PROPOSING TO GIRLFRIEND LYN-Z ADAMS HAWKINS TO KICK OFF OPENING NIGHT OF NITRO CIRCUS LIVE IN LAS VEGAS

maneuver from skateboarder Burnquist and a double front flip by BMXer **Andy Buckworth**.

It wasn't entirely good news at Nitro Circus, though. Motocross star **Levi Sherwood** was seriously injured when he tried to take off from a ramp and his bike shifted into neutral. In a scary scene, Sherwood was thrown off the bike in midair. He suffered multiple injuries and missed the rest of the Red Bull X-Fighters series in 2011, as well as Summer X Games 17 in Los Angeles.

SUMMER DEW TOUR 2010

CHAMPION	EVENT
Pierre-Luc Gagnon	Skate Vert
Chaz Ortiz	Skate Park
Daniel Dhers	BMX Park
Jamie Bestwick*	BMX Vert
Brandon Dosch	BMX Dirt

* Summer Dew Tour Athlete of the Year

Teen Sensation

Nyjah Huston dominated the regular portion of the Street League Skateboarding schedule in 2011. The 16-year-old won each of the three stops in Seattle, Kansas City, and Glendale, Arizona.

His performance earned him a trip to the winner-takes-all championship event in Newark, New Jersey, late in August. Huston and nine other top pros were to compete for $200,000—the largest purse in skateboarding history.

Rob Drydek's Street League debuted in 2010. Huston won the championship event that year when he nailed his final trick to edge out **Shane O'Neill** for the title.

Huston is a teen sensation in Street League.

Bad Break

American **Nate Adams** positioned himself for his third straight Red Bull X-Fighters season championship in 2011, but it came after a bad break for rival **André Villa** of Norway.

Villa, who narrowly missed out on the title in 2010, was in the lead heading into the next-to-last event of the freestyle motocross season, which was held in Poznan, Poland. During qualifying for that race, Villa broke his leg while doing a backflip.

Adams eventually won the competition before 40,000 fans in Poznan and moved into first place overall. Spain's **Dany Torres** also passed Villa and moved into second place overall.

WINTER X GAMES

FAMILIAR FACES

Many stars continued their recent run of success at the Winter X Games. **Shaun White** won the men's snowboard superpipe for the fourth year in a row. **Lindsey Jacobellis** made it four in a row, too, when she won the women's snowboarder X competition. **Tucker Hibbert** went one better when he won snowmobile snocross for the fifth year in a row.

Kelly Clark soars above the half-pipe.

A LITTLE HELP FROM A FRIEND

Levi LaVallee intended to ring in the new year in 2011 by soaring his snowmobile a world-record distance over a 300-foot water gap in San Diego. But he suffered serious injuries (including a collapsed lung and broken ribs) during a crash while practicing for the jump. That not only canceled LaVallee's New Year's Eve plans but also knocked him out of the Winter X Games in Aspen, Colorado, in January.

LaVallee still played a big role in the snowmobile best trick and freestyle events, however. He offered his facilities and sleds to help train Red Bull teammate **Daniel Bodin**, who went on to win gold in both competitions.

VICTORY LAP

Kelly Clark already had a gold medal wrapped up when she took her final run in the women's snowboard superpipe. But this is the X Games! So instead of playing it safe on her victory lap, she made history. She nailed a 1080—three full rotations off the pipe—the first woman ever to do it in competition.

SUMMER X GAMES

Traffic jam! The chaos of the Enduro X competition.

"'You could blow it right now or you could just win it.' I went with win it."

– **SHAUN WHITE**, RECOUNTING WHAT HE SAID TO HIMSELF BEFORE HIS WINNING RUN IN SKATE VERT

White Is Gold

Shaun White foiled **Pierre-Luc Gagnon**'s bid for a four-peat in skate vert with an amazing final run to rally from behind and win.

PLG took the lead by combining his usual technical precision with some stylish moves, too. But White came back with a near flawless run that wowed the judges and fans. He capped the routine with his signature trick, the "armadillo"—a front side heel flip 540 body varial.

Change of Plans

Travis Pastrana wanted to nail his "TP roll"—a 720 backflip combo—in the Moto X best trick competition at X Games 17 in Los Angeles. After that, he was going to jet to Indianapolis, Indiana, to make his debut in NASCAR's Nationwide Series. But Pastrana had to put off his Nationwide debut until 2012 after he broke his ankle in a crash.

Still, Pastrana amazed his fans when he got behind the wheel in rally car, anyway. His team rigged the car so that he controlled the accelerator with his hands instead of his right foot. He had a chance to win a medal, too, until he crashed and finished fourth.

News & Notes

➜ Enduro X debuted at X Games 17. Enduro is sort of a mix of supercross, trail riding—and chaos! **Taddy Blazusiak** and **Maria Forsberg** were the gold medalists.

➜ **Jamie Bestwick** took home the gold in BMX vert for the fifth year in a row. **Garrett Reynolds** won BMX street for the fourth time (all four years the event has been held in the X Games).

➜ From the Oh-By-the-Way Department: After Pastrana's injury, **Jackson Strong** won Moto X best trick by throwing down the first front flip in X Games competition.

2011 X GAMES WINNERS

Lindsey Jacobellis: snowboarder X gold in '08, '09, '10, and '11.

WINTER X GAMES 15 • Aspen, Colorado
January 27–30, 2011

Skiing Big Air
Alex Schlopy

Skiing Mono Skier X
Josh Deuck

Skiing Skier X (Men)
John Teller

Skiing Skier X (Women)
Kelsey Serwa

Skiing Slopestyle (Men)
Sammy Carlson

Skiing Slopestyle (Women)
Kaya Turski

Skiing SuperPipe (Men)
Kevin Rolland

Skiing SuperPipe (Women)
Sarah Burke

Snowboard Best Method
Scotty Lago

Snowboard Big Air
Torstein Horgmo

Snowboard Slopestyle (Men)
Sebastien Toutant

Snowboard Slopestyle (Women)
Enni Rukajarvi

Snowboard Snowboarder X (Men)
Nick Baumgartner

Snowboard Snowboarder X (Women)
Lindsey Jacobellis

Snowboard Street
Nic Sauve

Snowboard SuperPipe (Men)
Shaun White

Snowboard SuperPipe (Women)
Kelly Clark

Snowmobile Best Trick
Daniel Bodin

Snowmobile Freestyle
Daniel Bodin

Snowmobile SnoCross
Tucker Hibbert

Snowmobile SnoCross Adaptive
Mike Schultz

Snowmobile Speed & Style
Joe Parsons

SUMMER X GAMES 17 • Los Angeles, California
July 27–31, 2011

BMX Big Air
Steve McCann

BMX Street
Garrett Reynolds

BMX Park
Daniel Dhers

BMX Vert
Jamie Bestwick

Moto X Best Trick
Jackson Strong

Moto X Best Whip
Jeremy Stenberg

Moto X Enduro X (Men)
Taddy Blazusiak

Moto X Enduro X (Women)
Maria Forsberg

Moto X Freestyle
Nate Adams

Moto X Speed & Style
Nate Adams

Moto X Step Up
Matt Buyten

Moto X Racing (Women)
Vicki Golden

Rally Car Racing
Liam Doran

Nate Adams: two golds in 2011.

Rally Car RallyCross
Brian Deegan

Skate Big Air
Bob Burnquist

Skate Game of SK8
Ryan Decenzo

Skate Street (Men)
Nyjah Huston

Skate Street (Women)
Marisa Dal Santo

Skate Street (Amateur)
Julian Christianson

Skate Park
Raven Tershy

Skate Vert (Men)
Shaun White

Bob Burnquist gets some big air on his skateboard.

THE GOAL OF THE YEAR!
U.S. star Abby Wambach (20) slammed in this head ball with just seconds to spare against Brazil. The goal tied the score at 2–2 and gave the Americans a chance to win the World Cup quarterfinal game in a penalty-kick shoot-out.

20
3

SO CLOSE!

Watched by the biggest TV audience for any U.S. soccer game in history, the U.S. women's team came within a whisker of its third World Cup title. But in one of the most shocking upsets in the sport's history, Japan came from behind twice before beating the mighty American team in penalty kicks to win its first world championship.

The stunning loss was a tough end to a storybook tournament for the U.S. team. They came into it expecting to face Germany in the quarterfinals. But an opening-round loss to Sweden meant that the U.S. played Brazil instead. That soccer-crazy nation boasts **Marta**, the five-time World Player of the Year. After the U.S. battled back to tie the game, Marta worked her magic and scored an amazing goal to give Brazil a 2–1 lead in extra time. With time running out, wave after wave of American players tried to score the tying goal and force penalty kicks.

U.S. goalie Hope Solo shows the emotion that many felt on the field and at home.

Captain and star Homare Sawa holds up the World Cup trophy, won by Japan in a big upset.

All About Abby

Abby Wambach did all she could to put her team in a position to win. Her head-ball goals tied the game against Brazil and gave the U.S. leads against France and Japan. In the final shoot-out, she even made her penalty kick.

Wambach first got national notice while helping the University of Florida win the NCAA championship in 1998. She was also a three-time All-American there. She joined the U.S. national team in 2003. Her header gave the U.S. a win in the 2004 Olympic gold-medal game. At the 2007 World Cup, she scored six goals in six games, but then she had to miss the 2008 Olympics with a broken leg. She came back strong to join the new women's pro league in 2009, in which she was one of the top scorers.

With less than a minute left, **Megan Rapinoe** lofted a cross that **Abby Wambach** headed into the back of the net (see page 140). The dramatic goal set off a celebration across the U.S. In the penalty-kick shoot-out, goalie **Hope Solo** made a big save to help the U.S. advance.

In the semis, against France, Wambach's late header clinched the win again. Then it was on to the finals, where the U.S. would face Japan, which had knocked off Sweden and host nation Germany. The U.S. had never lost to Japan in 25 previous matchups.

However, the Japanese women were playing inspired soccer. Their homeland was still dealing with the effects of an earthquake and tsunami in March 2011. The athletes played to boost the spirits of their fellow Japanese. So even when the U.S. went ahead, 1–0, late in the game, the Japanese never gave up. They scored in the 80th minute to tie. Then, after yet another Wambach header to give the U.S. the lead, Japan scored in the 117th minute to tie the game. **Homare Sawa**, named the top player in the tournament, flicked in the goal. In the penalty kicks, a shocked U.S. team missed three kicks . . . and the Japanese made most of theirs. And Japan was the World Cup champion.

FINAL-ROUND GAMES

QUARTERFINALS

France 1*, England 1
U.S. 2*, Brazil 2
Japan 1, Germany 0
Sweden 3, Australia 1

SEMIFINALS

U.S. 2, France 1
Japan 3, Sweden 1

CHAMPIONSHIP GAME

Japan 2, U.S. 2**

* Advanced on penalty kicks ** Won on penalty kicks

MARVELOUS MESSI

Messi shows off the moves that make him the world's best player.

Everyone already knew that **Lionel Messi** is the best player in the world. He had been named that after the 2009 and 2010 seasons. But even those amazing years did not prepare fans for what he accomplished in 2011. Messi was simply magical. In games for his club team, Barcelona, he scored an amazing 51 goals, plus had 22 assists. And while the goals came in bunches, it was how he scored them that was even more impressive. His goal in a 2–0 win over Manchester United in the UEFA Champions League final was a thing of beauty. He faked out three defenders in the space of about 15 feet, then toe-poked the ball into the far side of the net past the diving goalie.

Led by Messi, Barcelona won La Liga, the Spanish national league. Then it won the Champions League over Man U, in a thriller of a game watched by hundreds of millions of fans worldwide.

Other World Soccer Results

LEAGUE	COUNTRY	CHAMPION
Premier League	England	Manchester United
Ligue 1	France	Lille
Bundesliga	Germany	Borussia Dortmund
Serie A	Italy	AC Milan
La Liga	Spain	FC Barcelona
Série A	Brazil	Fluminese*
Primera Division	Mexico	Tigres
J-League	Japan	Nagoya Grampus*

* 2010 champion; all others 2010–11 or 2011

MLS REPORT

The Colorado Rapids came into the 2010 MLS play-offs ranked seventh out of the top eight teams. The team had not made it to the MLS Cup championship game since 1997. So perhaps only their fans were not surprised when the Rapids walked away with the title after defeating FC Dallas, 2–1.

The teams were tied, 1–1, after the first 90 minutes, and then the game turned on a wild play in the 17th minute of overtime. Colorado's **Macoumba Kandji** smacked a ball toward the Dallas goal. Defender **George John** stuck out his leg to block the shot . . . but the ball bounced off John and past goalie **Kevin Hartman**! The Rapids held on for a few more minutes to win their first MLS championship.

Captain Pablo Mastroeni led Colorado.

Chris Wondolowski of the San Jose Earthquakes won the Golden Boot award after leading the league with 18 goals. In one stretch, he scored 10 straight goals! **Donovan Ricketts** of the L.A. Galaxy was chosen the top goalie. He set a team record with 11 shutouts while helping the Galaxy end up ranked first in the regular-season standings.

Looking ahead, the big news around MLS is the arrival of two new teams. The Portland Timbers and the Vancouver Whitecaps began play in 2011. In 2012, another new team, the Montreal Impact, will become MLS's 19th team and the 3rd from Canada.

2010 MLS FINAL STANDINGS

EASTERN CONFERENCE	POINTS
New York Red Bulls	51
Columbus Crew	50
Kansas City Wizards	39
Chicago Fire	36
Toronto FC	35
New England Revolution	32
Philadelphia Union	31
D.C. United	22

WESTERN CONFERENCE	POINTS
Los Angeles Galaxy	59
Real Salt Lake	56
FC Dallas	50
Seattle Sounders FC	48
Colorado Rapids	46
San Jose Earthquakes	46
Houston Dynamo	33
Chivas USA	28

QUICK KICKS!

Americans in England

More and more Americans have been playing in England's Premier League in the past decade or so. In 2011, **Stuart Holden** was named the MVP for Bolton. **Tim Howard** plays for Everton and is one of the top goalies in the league. And in March, forward **Clint Dempsey** scored his 10th goal of the season for Fulham, the most ever for a U.S. player in England.

COPA AMERICA Every four years, the nations of South America battle to claim the Copa America title. The 2011 Copa was held in stadiums in Argentina. The host country, along with tournament favorite Brazil, went out early. In the end, the final was between a pair of surprises: Paraguay and Uruguay. With a 3–0 victory, Uruguay took home the Copa.

GOLD CUP

The Gold Cup is played every four years by teams in North and Central America. The U.S. and Mexico nearly always end up in the final game. In 2011, however, Panama gave the U.S. its first-ever loss in the opening round. The Americans rebounded to beat Guadaloupe and advance to the quarterfinals. Meanwhile, Mexico was rolling, scoring 16 goals in its first four games, including a hat trick against El Salvador by star forward **Javier Hernandez**.

In the semifinals, a late score by **Clint Dempsey** after a perfect pass from **Landon Donovan** gave the U.S. revenge for their earlier loss to Panama. That set up the expected U.S. vs. Mexico championship game.

In the final, the U.S. went up, 2–0, after only 23 minutes. But the powerful and talented Mexican team swarmed back. Mexico scored the last four goals of the match and won, 4–2. The final goal came on a perfectly placed, swerving kick by **Giovani Dos Santos**.

Dos Santos battles Michael Bradley.

What a Goal!

The awesome English forward **Wayne Rooney** scored one of the most amazing goals of recent years. He flipped backward in a bicycle kick that scored the winning goal in Manchester United's big rivalry game with Manchester City. "It was stunning," said longtime Man U coach **Alex Ferguson**. "We've had some fantastic goals here, but in terms of execution, you'll never see better."

The goal gave United a 2–1 victory on their way to winning their 17th Premier League title, tying Liverpool for the most ever.

Players to Watch

Keep an eye out for these young international stars:

✷ **Neymar**, Brazil/Santos ▶▶▶
Another in a long line of talented Brazilians, Neymar will probably bring his talents to a European team soon.

✷ **Javier Hernandez**, Mexico/Man. United: Known as Chicarito, "Little Pea," Hernandez was a perfect partner for the bruising Wayne Rooney on Man U's championship team.

✷ **Jack Wilshere**, England/Arsenal
A great hope for England's future, Wilshere is very fast and will surely make his mark on the world soccer stage.

✷ **Manuel Neuer**, Germany/Bayern Munich
One of the best young goalies in the world, Neuer has a bright future with the German national squad.

STAT STUFF

MAJOR LEAGUE SOCCER CHAMPIONS

2010	Colorado Rapids
2009	Real Salt Lake
2008	Columbus Crew
2007	Houston Dynamo
2006	Houston Dynamo
2005	Los Angeles Galaxy
2004	D.C. United
2003	San Jose Earthquakes
2002	Los Angeles Galaxy
2001	San Jose Earthquakes
2000	Kansas City Wizards
1999	D.C. United
1998	Chicago Fire
1997	D.C. United
1996	D.C. United

World Cup Scoring Leaders

MEN

GOALS	PLAYER, COUNTRY
15	Ronaldo, Brazil
14	Miroslav Klose, Germany
14	Gerd Müller, West Germany
13	Just Fontaine, France
12	Pelé, Brazil
11	Jürgen Klinsmann, Germany
11	Sandor Kocsis, Hungary

WOMEN

GOALS	PLAYER, COUNTRY
14	Birgit Prinz, Germany
14	Marta, Brazil
13	Abby Wambach, United States
12	Michelle Akers, United States

WOMEN'S WORLD CUP
ALL-TIME RESULTS

YEAR	CHAMPION	RUNNER-UP
2011	**Japan**	United States
2007	**Germany**	Brazil
2003	**Germany**	Sweden
1999	**United States**	China
1995	**Norway**	Germany
1991	**United States**	Norway

This goal, scored by Brandi Chastain of the U.S., gave the Americans the 1991 World Cup title.

RORY'S THE STORY

Whether he won or lost, **Rory McIlroy** was the big story in golf in 2011.

At the Masters in April, the 21-year-old from Northern Ireland thrilled the golfing world by fashioning a four-stroke lead heading into the final round. He struggled early but still clung to a one-shot lead after the ninth hole. Then the roof fell in. He hit two drives out-of-bounds, had trouble putting, and ended up shooting 80 for the day. He finished tied for 15th place.

Meanwhile, all around McIlroy, the rest of the field was putting on one of the best final rounds in Masters history. At one point **Tiger Woods** (remember him?) was tied for the lead. Several other golfers made a run at the top, including **Luke Donald**, **Jason Day**, and **Adam Scott**. The steady play of **Charl Schwartzel** rose to the top. He ran off 10 straight pars, then he made 4 straight birdies to finish his round. He was the first South African since **Ernie Els** to win the famous green jacket.

After the Masters, many fans worried that the collapse would hurt young McIlroy. Could he bounce back from such a rough day?

Um, yes.

At the U.S. Open in June, McIlroy put on the most dominating performance in the 111-year history of the event. The Open is regarded by most experts as the most difficult major in which to post a low score. McIlroy proved them wrong by shooting four rounds under 70. His total score of 268 was the lowest ever . . . by 4 strokes! He won by 8 strokes, one of the biggest margins ever. He also became the youngest U.S. Open champion since **Bobby Jones** way back in 1923. By "Rory-ing" back from his Masters disaster, McIlroy has put himself firmly atop the golf world.

2011 MAJOR WINNERS

THE MASTERS
Charl Schwartzel

THE U.S. OPEN
Rory McIlroy

THE BRITISH OPEN
Darren Clarke

THE PGA CHAMPIONSHIP
Keegan Bradley

A WINNER'S SMILE
With a terrific golf stroke and a maturity that seems older than his 21 years, Rory McIlroy turned the golf world on its head in 2011.

CHIP SHOTS

BIG MONEY!

Jim Furyk cruised home with one of the biggest paydays in golf history in September 2010. For winning the Tour Championship, a single tournament, he was awarded $1.35 million. He also booked enough points to clinch the season-ending FedEx Cup competition, which is held over three tournaments. For the FedEx Cup championship, he received a check for $10 million!

CLOSE CALL!

Every two years, the best golfers in the United States face a team from Europe (below). The winning team gets the Ryder Cup. The sport changes from a battle between individuals to a contest between teams. In October 2010, the Ryder Cup was not decided until the final match of the three-day event, in one of the most exciting finishes in its 83-year history.

Europe led by three points after the second day of the event. The final day had 12 singles matches. It was actually a day late, on a Monday, thanks to a rainstorm that soaked the course in Wales. The Europeans needed only 5 points out of that final 12 to capture the Ryder Cup. Thanks to some great comebacks by American golfers **Tiger Woods**, **Phil Mickelson**, and **Rickie Fowler**, the U.S. team made it superclose. The Cup came down to the final match between Ireland's **Graeme McDowell** and America's **Hunter Mahan**. McDowell held on to win by one hole (in singles play, golfers try to win each hole, not post the lowest overall score). The final score was a squeaker, 14.5–13.5. It was Europe's first win since 2006.

TV Refs?

Golf fans watch their heroes closely . . . and golfers had better watch out. Twice in 2011, TV viewers sent e-mails that cost pro golfers penalty strokes. How did they do that? While watching at home, the fans saw the golfers do things wrong. **Padraig Harrington** was caught moving his ball while removing a dropped coin near the ball. It cost him two penalty strokes after the round was over. In Hawaii, **Camilo Villegas** (left) was disqualified from an event after a viewer reported that Villegas had moved some loose grass.

"It's all a blur."

That's what golfer **Kevin Na** said after one of the worst days ever on the PGA Tour. Bad drives, missed chips, bad bounces, and just bad luck helped him record a 16 on the par-4 ninth hole. Na, playing in the Texas Open, just kept swinging and trying . . . 16 times! It was the highest single-hole score since **John Daly**'s 18 in 1998.

Now That's What We Call a Partner!

A pair of American military men got a special treat in February. **Lt. Col. Michael Rowells** (below, with **Tiger Woods**) and **Specialist Huey Hughes** got to take part in a special golf tournament with Woods. Rowells won the spot in a drawing for servicemen. He brought along Hughes as his caddy. The two men got a break from serving in Afghanistan for the unique golf holiday. "It was the opportunity of a lifetime," said Hughes. For Woods, it was a way to honor his late father, **Earl**, who had a long military career.

LPGA NEWS

ANOTHER STAR RISES

The best women's golfer in the world was little known in the U.S. when the 2010 LPGA season opened. By the end of it, there was no one in the sport who did not know about **Yani Tseng**. In 2010, the native of Taiwan won two majors—the British Open and the Kraft Nabisco—and finished fourth in earnings. She ended up becoming the first player from Taiwan—and second youngest—to win the Rolex Player of the Year award. In early 2011, she took over the top spot in the world rankings, and her play kept her there all year.

She added a runaway victory in the LPGA Championship in June 2011. Her score of 19 under par tied a record for any LPGA major tournament. Then she won her second British Open in July. She became the youngest player ever to total five majors in her career.

Tseng rises to the top at the best events—of her nine LPGA Tour wins, five have been majors! She has won tournaments in Thailand, Taiwan, and Australia. The bad news for her LPGA rivals? Tseng is only 22!

Tseng is part of an ongoing rush of athletes from Asia who are dominating the women's pro circuit. The 2010 top money winner was **Na Yeon Choi** from South Korea. Midway through 2011, 6 of the top 10 golfers on the world rankings list were from Asia . . . and only 2, **Cristie Kerr** and **Paula Creamer**, were from the United States.

Kerr has been the top American golfer for several years. Midway through 2011, she had finished in the top 10 of 7 of her 10 starts, and she was No. 2 on the money list. Kerr has 14 victories in her stellar seven-year LPGA career.

"She hits it really long out there, and she plays with a lot of flair. It's fun to watch."

— CRISTIE KERR
ON YANI TSENG

One of the longest hitters on the tour, Tseng is ready to stay on top for a long time!

2011 LPGA Majors

Kraft Nabisco Championship: **Stacy Lewis**

LPGA Championship: **Yani Tseng**

◀◀◀ U.S. Women's Open: **So Yeon Ryu**

Women's British Open: **Yani Tseng**

LPGA Money Winners

Top earners on the 2010 LPGA Tour

1. **Na Yeon Choi**	$1.87 million
2. **Jiyai Shin**	$1.78 million
3. **Cristie Kerr**	$1.60 million
4. **Suzann Pettersen**	$1.55 million
5. **Yani Tseng**	$1.53 million

GIVING BACK

The RR Donnelley LPGA Founders Cup offered the players $1 million in prize money . . . but when it was all over, the players didn't get a dime. Instead, in a unique form of sportsmanship and sharing, all of the players donated their winnings to their favorite charities. The LPGA gave half of the money to the LPGA-USGA Girls Golf program, while players chose where the rest went. Tournament winner **Karrie Webb**, for instance, had her $200,000 prize sent to help earthquake and tsunami victims in Japan as well as to a group that helps victims of spinal injuries. Other golfers sent money to help animals, international aid groups, and people with eating disorders.

THE MAJORS

In golf, some tournaments are known as the majors. They're the four most important events of the year on either the men's or the women's pro tours. **Tiger Woods** has the most career wins in majors among current golfers. **Annika Sorenstam** retired in 2010 with the most among recent LPGA players.

MEN'S

	MASTERS	U.S. OPEN	BRITISH OPEN	PGA CHAMP.	TOTAL
Jack **NICKLAUS**	6	4	3	5	**18**
Tiger **WOODS**	4	3	3	4	**14**
Walter **HAGEN**	0	2	4	5	**11**
Ben **HOGAN**	2	4	1	2	**9**
Gary **PLAYER**	3	1	3	2	**9**
Tom **WATSON**	2	1	5	0	**8**
Arnold **PALMER**	4	1	2	0	**7**
Gene **SARAZEN**	1	2	1	3	**7**
Sam **SNEAD**	3	0	1	3	**7**
Harry **VARDON**	0	1	6	0	**7**

ARNOLD PALMER

Few athletes in any sport have been as popular for as long as Palmer has. He rose to the top of the golfing world in the mid-1950s. He was not a rich country-club guy—he grew up playing at public courses. Fans followed him from tournament to tournament, forming "Arnie's Army" at courses around the country. Palmer also helped bring U.S. golfers back to the British Open when he won it 1961. Though retired from active play, he remains a popular spokesman for products and companies and a great ambassador for the sport.

WOMEN'S

	LPGA	USO	BO	NAB	MAUR	TH	WES	TOTAL
Patty **BERG**	0	1	x	x	x	7	7	15
Mickey **WRIGHT**	4	4	x	x	x	2	3	13
Louise **SUGGS**	1	2	x	x	x	4	4	11
Annika **SORENSTAM**	3	3	1	3	x	x	x	10
Babe **ZAHARIAS**	x	3	x	x	x	3	4	10
Betsy **RAWLS**	2	4	x	x	x	x	2	8
Juli **INKSTER**	2	2	x	2	1	x	x	7
Karrie **WEBB**	1	2	1	2	1	x	x	7

KEY: LPGA = LPGA Championship, USO = U.S. Open, BO = British Open, NAB = Nabisco Championship, MAUR = du Maurier (1979–2000), TH = Titleholders (1937–1972), WES = Western Open (1937–1967)

PGA TOUR CAREER EARNINGS*

1. Tiger Woods $94,728,667
2. Vijay Singh $64,852,519
3. Phil Mickelson $62,863,910
4. Jim Furyk $48,359,276
5. Davis Love III $41,086,053
6. Ernie Els $40,745,845
7. David Toms $36,269,990
8. Kenny Perry $31,695,792
9. Steve Stricker $31,164,279
10. Justin Leonard $30,717,357

LPGA TOUR CAREER EARNINGS*

1. Annika Sorenstam $22,573,192
2. Karrie Webb $16,299,291
3. Lorena Ochoa $14,863,331
4. Juli Inkster $13,269,656
5. Cristie Kerr $12,776,923

* Through July 2011

Nancy Lopez

Nancy Lopez was one of the top female golfers of the 1980s. She got off to a hot start, winning both the Rookie of the Year and the Player of the Year awards in 1978 (she went on to win three more Player of the Year awards). But she was more than just a 48-tournament winner (including 3 majors). Her Hispanic heritage—and her big smile and bubbly personality—made her a hero for many young Americans, male and female. Meanwhile, she was a leader in a growing movement to get more girls involved in sports. She has received numerous awards for her work off the golf course.

TENNIS

THE NEW BOSS!
An amazing win streak and a powerful all-around game sent Novak Djokovic rocketing to the top of the tennis world.

HE'S NO DJOK!

The tennis world has been waiting for someone to come along to break up the one-two combo of **Rafael Nadal** and **Roger Federer**. That duo had won just about all of the big events for many years. In 2011, fans got their wish. **Novak Djokovic** (JOKE-oh-vik) put together one of the best streaks of success of all time. He won 41 matches in a row to start the 2011 season, the second-longest streak ever at the beginning of a year. (Including 2010, he won 43 in a row, three short of the all-time record.) A semifinal win at Wimbledon (on his way to a championship-match victory over Nadal) made Djokovic the No. 1 player in the world. Nadal had held the top spot for just over a year, while Federer had been on top before that, all the way back to 2004.

Rafael Nadal lost his top spot to the Serbian star.

Included in Djokovic's amazing streak were victories at the Australian Open and Wimbledon, giving him a total of three Grand Slam championships. While he's still far short of Federer (an all-time record 16) and Nadal (10) in that category, Djokovic is now on top of the tennis world. He also won six events on the ATP World Tour in the first half of the year.

Now that he's famous, you might want to know a little more about him.

* He's the first player from Serbia to rank No. 1.
* His parents own a pizza restaurant on a mountain in Serbia.
* He comes from an athletic family—his father, uncle, and aunt were all professional skiers.
* He speaks four languages: Serbian, Italian, German, and English.

In other men's tennis news, Nadal continues to move up the list of the greatest players ever. With a victory over Federer in the French Open final, he tied for 6th all time in Grand Slam events won. And he's actually four years younger than Federer was when the Swiss star won his 10th.

A great duo atop men's tennis? Make that a great trio!

2011 GRAND SLAM WINNERS (MEN)

AUSTRALIAN OPEN	**Novak Djokovic**
FRENCH OPEN	**Rafael Nadal**
WIMBLEDON	**Novak Djokovic**
U.S. OPEN	**Novak Djokovic**

NEW FACES!

Li Na made history with her win at the French Open.

Women's tennis has been dominated in recent years by American stars **Serena** and **Venus Williams** and by a string of powerful players from Russia. Lots of things changed in 2011, however, and a set of new faces emerged on the world scene.

At the Australian Open, one familiar face did win. **Kim Clijsters** from Belgium, coming off her 2010 U.S. Open win, won Down Under. It was her fourth Grand Slam title. In the final, she beat an up-and-coming player from China, **Li Na**, who would soon make her own mark on history.

Several weeks after the Australian Open, Li became the first player from China—or even from Asia—to win a Grand Slam event when she captured the French Open. Cheers echoed over the famous red clay in Paris as Li beat Italy's **Francesca Schiavone**.

This Wimbledon trophy might not be the last for the hard-hitting Petra Kvitova.

It turned out that losing the Australian Open final set Li up for winning the French.

"I had no experience," she said in Paris, about her time in Australia. "I was very nervous. [At the French,] for my second time in a final, I had the experience. I knew how to do it. And I had more self-confidence."

At the third Grand Slam of the year, another new winner was crowned. At Wimbledon in June, **Petra Kvitova**, a hard-hitting lefty from the Czech Republic, smashed her way to her first Grand Slam title. She beat **Maria Sharapova** in just 85 minutes. Kvitova's powerful shots were perfect for the grass courts at Wimbledon.

Kvitova grew up idolizing another left-handed player from her home country. **Martina Navratilova** was one of the greatest players ever, with 18 Grand Slams among her record 167 tournament victories.

In 2010, Serena Williams was named the

WHERE ARE THE AMERICANS?

Thanks to the injury to **Serena Williams**, which dropped her out of the top of the rankings, American tennis took a big hit. In May 2011, for the first time ever, no American tennis players were in the top 10 of either the men's or the women's rankings. (Plus, at Wimbledon for the first time since 1913, all of the top 8 women's players were from Europe.) The good news is that by July, **Mardy Fish** (left) and **Andy Roddick** had slipped back into the top 10. **Venus Williams** was the highest-ranked U.S. women's player, at No. 34.

top player of 2010 by ESPN, thanks to her win at Wimbledon. But not long after that, she stepped on broken glass at a restaurant. The resulting injury to her foot kept her off the court for months. When she was ready to come back, she became ill and couldn't play until summer. However, she battled back and, in July, won her first tournament since Wimbledon at the Bank of the West Classic in California. With her return and the rise of new stars, women's tennis should be strong in 2012.

2011 GRAND SLAM WINNERS (WOMEN)

AUSTRALIAN OPEN	**Kim Clijsters**
FRENCH OPEN	**Li Na**
WIMBLEDON	**Petra Kvitova**
U.S. OPEN	**Samantha Stosur**

Early Out for the U.S.

Feliciano Lopez beat Mardy Fish of the U.S.

Even with Spanish superstar **Rafael Nadal** out of the lineup, the U.S. could not beat Spain's team in the Davis Cup. In July, Spain knocked the U.S. out of the international competition in the quarterfinals. Meanwhile, with the help of **Novak Djokovic**, Serbia was moving up. The Serbian team won its first Davis Cup in 2010 and was in the semifinals in 2011.

STAT STUFF

ALL-TIME GRAND SLAM CHAMPIONSHIPS (MEN)

	AUS. OPEN	FRENCH OPEN	WIMBLEDON	U.S. OPEN	TOTAL
Roger **FEDERER**	4	1	6	5	16
Pete **SAMPRAS**	2	0	7	5	14
Roy **EMERSON**	6	2	2	2	12
Björn **BORG**	0	6	5	0	11
Rod **LAVER**	3	2	4	2	11
Rafael **NADAL**	1	6	2	1	10
Bill **TILDEN**	0	0	3	7	10
Jimmy **CONNORS**	1	0	2	5	8
Ivan **LENDL**	2	3	0	3	8
Fred **PERRY**	1	1	3	3	8
Ken **ROSEWALL**	4	2	0	2	8
Andre **AGASSI**	4	1	1	2	8

JIMMY CONNORS

Fiery and hard fighting, Connors dominated men's tennis in the 1970s. He was No. 1 in the world from 1974–1978 and won three U.S. Opens in the decade (he added two more in the 1980s). His powerful left-handed stroke made almost as much noise as his regular arguments with officials. As he grew older, however, he mellowed out, but he still played great tennis. He won the last of his eight Grand Slam events at the 1983 U.S. Open. Connors also holds the record for the most tournament victories, with 109.

ALL-TIME GRAND SLAM CHAMPIONSHIPS (WOMEN)

	AUS.	FRENCH	WIMBLEDON	U.S.	TOTAL
Margaret Smith **COURT**	11	5	3	5	**24**
Steffi **GRAF**	4	6	7	5	**22**
Helen Wills **MOODY**	0	4	8	7	**19**
Chris **EVERT**	2	7	3	6	**18**
Martina **NAVRATILOVA**	3	2	9	4	**18**
Serena **WILLIAMS**	5	1	4	3	**13**
Billie Jean **KING**	1	1	6	4	**12**
Maureen **CONNOLLY**	1	2	3	3	**9**
Monica **SELES**	4	3	0	2	**9**
Suzanne **LENGLEN**	0	2*	6	0	**8**
Molla Bjurstedt **MALLORY**	0	0	0	8	**8**

* Also won 4 French titles before 1925; in those years, the tournament was open only to French nationals.

HELEN WILLS MOODY

Novak Djokovic had a pretty good winning streak in 2011 (see page 158). But he'll have to keep it up until *2018* to beat the 180-match, seven-year streak of Helen Wills Moody. She was the top women's tennis player in the world in the 1920s and 1930s, winning 19 Grand Slam events. She also won gold medals in singles and doubles at the 1924 Olympics, plus 12 Grand Slam doubles championships. Her powerful game made her the first American woman to be an international sports star.

LOCHTE

OTHER SPORTS

NEXT STOP: LONDON

American swimmer Ryan Lochte won five gold medals and set a world record at the 2011 World Aquatics Championships. Olympic star Michael Phelps added four more. They'll head a powerful U.S. team as it gets ready for the next Summer Olympics in London in 2012.

Under a last-minute jockey, Animal Kingdom raced to a Kentucky Derby win.

HORSE RACING

Animal Kingdom had never run a race on dirt before the 2011 Kentucky Derby. The jockey riding him, **John Velazquez**, almost didn't have a horse to ride in the same race: His first mount was cut from the field due to an injury. But when the two got together the day before the race, they turned into champions. Animal Kingdom was the surprise winner of the big race at Churchill Downs. It was the first time in the 137 years of the derby that a horse won in its first race on dirt. Animal Kingdom's earlier races had been on grass.

The Kentucky Derby is just the first of the "three jewels" of the Triple Crown. At the Preakness, the second race, Animal Kingdom nearly made it two in a row. The Derby winner started slowly, trailing the field. But halfway through the race in Baltimore, Animal Kingdom made an amazing charge toward the lead. However, he didn't have enough to catch the winner, **Shackelford**.

"We were just too far back," Velazquez said. "When I wanted him to go, he got dirt kicked in his face. By the time I had the chance to go, it was too late."

The win by Shackelford meant that there again would be no Triple Crown winner in 2011. The last horse to win all three races in one year was **Affirmed**, in 1978.

At the Belmont Stakes, Animal Kingdom struggled again, almost tripping. Velazquez's foot also came out of a stirrup. By the time they gathered themselves together, it was too late. Meanwhile, **Ruler on Ice** was staying close to the lead, waiting for the right moment. With a rush at the end, the long shot won his first major race.

TRACK AND FIELD

At the 2011 USA Outdoor Track & Field Championships, most athletes were thinking about the days ahead . . . but some were also thinking a *year* ahead. The ultimate goal for many of the Americans at the event in Eugene, Oregon, was the Summer Olympics set for London in 2012. Some of the highlights of the U.S. meet:

- ★ **Walter Dix** took gold in both the 100- and 200-meter sprints. ▶▶▶
- ★ **Allyson Felix**, a former Olympic gold medalist, won her specialty, the 400 meters.
- ★ **Nick Symmonds** won his fourth national title in the 800 meters, and **Alysia Montano** won her third.
- ★ Both 1500-meter races ended with runners on the track after tripping or crashing. In the women's race, defending champ **Christin Wurth-Thomas** slowed and **Morgan Uceny** passed her near the finish line. Several runners actually crashed behind Uceny. In the men's race, **Matt Centrowitz** won his first title, holding off former Olympic medalist **Bernard Lagat**. That race, too, had a couple of crashes. "It was ugly out there," said runner **Evan Jager**.
- ★ **Jesse Williams** set a U.S. meet record in the high jump, soaring 7 feet, 9⅓ inches.

MARATHON PEOPLE

At the 2011 Boston Marathon, **Geoffrey Mutai** (left) of Kenya ran the fastest marathon of all time . . . 2:03:02. He won by four seconds, and he beat the all-time mark by nearly a minute. One problem: Mutai's amazing feat doesn't count as a world record. The Boston Marathon course is too downhill to qualify its runners for records.

American runners had a good day in Boston, too. **Ryan Hall**'s 2:04:58 was the fastest ever by a U.S. runner. **Desiree Davila** finished second to Kenya's **Caroline Kilel** by only two seconds.

Top cowboy Brazile shows 'em the ropes!

RODEO

COWBOYS

Trevor Brazile continues to be America's top all-around cowboy. By winning the Professional Rodeo Cowboys Association national championship in 2010 (and holding a commanding lead in 2011), he continued a decade of dominance. In 2010, he was tops in two categories—tie-down roping and team roping—and second in steer roping. Late in the 2011 season, he had won nearly three times as much money as **Shane Proctor**, who was in second place in the all-around category.

BULL RIDERS

While the top cowboy is Brazile, the top bull rider is from Brazil! **Renato Nunes** won the 2010 Professional Bull Riders tour. It took an awesome performance at the World Finals for Nunes to end up on top. He successfully rode five of six bulls and rose from third to first on the final day. He started riding bulls when he was 18, back home in Brazil. He joined the PBR in 2005 and steadily worked his way to the top in this dangerous and exciting sport.

Nunes wasn't alone in 2011, however. Late in the season, after Nunes went out with an injury, the top three riders were a trio of other Brazilian stars.

LACROSSE

Indoors or outdoors, lacrosse is one of the fastest-growing sports in the U.S. More and more schools are adding teams, while youth leagues can be found from California to Texas to North Carolina.

At the pro level, the National Lacrosse League plays indoors. The Toronto Rock (in white at right) won their second league title in 2011, defeating the Washington Stealth.

Major League Lacrosse is home to the best outdoor players in the country. Their summer 2011 season ended in late August with the Boston Cannons winning their first championship.

Batsman M. S. Dhoni hit the winning runs for India.

CRICKET

You might not have seen this event, but more than a billion people around the world were enthralled by it. The Cricket World Cup was played in India in April 2011. Fourteen countries sent teams to compete. For the first time ever, the host country won the championship. India beat Sri Lanka in the final, setting off a nationwide celebration in a country that loves cricket as much as the U.S. loves football and baseball.

Cricket is somewhat similar to baseball, with a pitcher (called a bowler) and a batter, but with only two bases and more fielders.

GYMNASTICS

At the 2010 World Gymnastics Championships in the Netherlands, American athletes put on quite a show, bringing home six major medals. Only one was gold, but with the 2012 Olympics coming up, it was a good showing for both the men's and women's teams. The women's team did especially well, capturing the team silver to go with **Rebecca Bross**'s three individual medals.

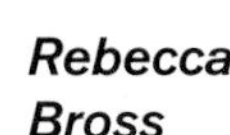

Rebecca Bross

CYCLING

Cadel Evans became the first Australian ever to win the Tour de France. To the delight of his many Aussie fans, Evans used a time trial late in the monthlong event to snatch the title. He went into the 26.4-mile race 57 seconds behind leader **Andy Schleck**. Evans made up all that and more, riding the course 2 minutes and 31 seconds faster! The Tour de France has been pedaling around Europe for 108 years, and only a few riders from outside that continent have won. At 34, Evans was also the oldest Tour de France winner in 89 years.

Earlier in the race, several big crashes took out some top riders. French rider **Thomas Voeckler** thrilled home-country fans when he wore the yellow jersey of the leader for nearly two weeks. However, the veteran rider was so sure that someone would catch him that at one point late in the race, he simply said, "No, there is no way I can win."

Cadel Evans

BOXING

Klitschko (right) dominated the talkative Haye.

The biggest boxing match of the year turned out to be pretty boring. Heavyweight champion **Wladimir Klitschko** of Ukraine took on **David Haye** from England. Haye talked a big game before the fight, but once the fight started, he spent most of his time avoiding the big champ. All three fight judges gave the win to Klitschko by wide margins. The victory gave the Ukrainian the championship in four of the five major international boxing organizations. The fifth is held by his brother **Vitali**. But don't look for the brothers to fight anytime soon: They both promised their mother they wouldn't box against each other!

The other big fight of the year saw **Manny Pacquiao** defeat **Sugar Shane Mosley** in Las Vegas. Though fans were happy to see Pacquiao fight, they still waited for him to take on **Floyd Mayweather**. Those two fighters are seen as the best in the world in any weight class, but they haven't faced each other yet.

FISHING

Kevin VanDam won his fourth Bassmaster Classic title in February. Fishing at Lake Cataouatche near New Orleans, VanDam won, with a three-day total of 69 pounds, 11 ounces of fish. That was about 10 pounds more than the second-place finisher. VanDam became the first angler to top $5 million in career earnings.

WINTER SPORTS

Vonn won two titles but missed in all-around.

SKIING

American skier **Lindsey Vonn** had won three straight World Cup overall championships. Coming into the final race of the 2011 season, it looked like she had a shot at an amazing fourth. She trailed the leader, **Maria Riesch** of Germany. But you need one thing for a ski race: snow. The morning of the final event, race officials declared that conditions on the course in Switzerland were not good enough to race, so the final event was called off.

Just like that, Vonn's chance for title number four was gone. Based on the points earned up to that time, Riesch was declared the champion. She won her first World Cup overall title only three points ahead of Vonn.

FIGURE SKATING

The sport of ice dancing has been dominated by skaters from other countries, notably Russia and Canada. But Americans **Meryl Davis** and **Charlie White** (right) changed that at the 2011 World Figure Skating Championships in Moscow. They became the first team ever from the U.S. to win gold in the graceful event.

In the women's individual event, **Kim Yu-Na** of South Korea, the defending champ, was upset by Japan's **Miki Ando**. The top U.S. skater was **Alissa Czisny**, who finished fifth.

For the men, **Patrick Chan** of Canada not only won gold, he set a new world record for points in the event.

Ligety was the World Cup slalom champ.

"Win or lose, I just wanted the chance," said Vonn after the decision was announced. "I feel devastated."

Though she lost the overall title, Vonn did win the world super-G, downhill, and combined titles to add to her amazing résumé as the most successful American ski racer ever.

On the men's side, **Ivica Kostelic** of Croatia was the overall World Cup champ. It was his first World Cup title and the first ever by a Croatian. He won two individual event championships as well. In ninth place, **Ted Ligety** was the best American racer.

The World Cup is a season-long competition that includes many races in many places. Every two years, however, a World Championship is held in one location, with the top racers trying to win their specialties.

At the 2011 event, held in Germany, Austria came home with eight medals, the most of any country, including four of the five golds in the women's races. American skiers earned a total of three medals.

IDITAROD

John Baker won the Iditarod, the grueling dogsled race across Alaska. What made Baker's victory, his first after 16 tries, extra-special was that he was the first Eskimo to win the event. Alaskan natives celebrated his feat with a display of drumming during the final laps of the race in Nome, Alaska. The Iditarod tests drivers and dogs, who travel 1,150 miles across frozen lands and dense, snow-covered forests. Baker covered the distance in just over 8 days and 18 hours.

SWIMMING

American swimmer **Michael Phelps** dominated the 2008 Olympics, winning an amazing eight gold medals. But he was not satisfied and is eyeing more in 2012. On the way there, he took part in the 2011 World Aquatics Championships, held in Shanghai in July. While Phelps did win four golds at the event, he was not the biggest American star. **Ryan Lochte** set a world record in the 200-meter individual medley (a race in which competitors swim 50 meters in each of four different strokes). That gave Lochte one of the five gold medals he won at the event. His record was a big deal in more ways than one: It was the first by any swimmer since the superfast bodysuits used at the 2008 Games were banned from the sport.

U.S. Women: Gold at the Worlds

SWIMMER	EVENT
Dana VOLLMER	100 fly
Rebecca SONI	100 breast
TEAM	4x200 freestyle relay
Missy FRANKLIN	200 breast
TEAM	4x100 medley relay
Jessica HARDY	50 free
Elizabeth BEISEL	400 individual medley

Besides the relays, Phelps and Lochte were the only American men to win gold. The women's team, however, racked up quite a haul (see above). Their success could mean good things ahead in London.

The host country got a big surprise on the final day. **Sun Yang** won the 1,500-meter swim in a world record time. He beat a mark that had stood for 10 years.

China's Sun rose at home.

OUTSIDE THE OLYMPICS

With the Summer Olympics coming up in London in 2012, many of the world's top athletes used other international events to get ready. Here's a wrap-up of two recent Olympic-like festivals of sport.

Dan was the man in China.

Asian Games

More than 10,000 athletes from 45 countries all over Asia came to Guanzhou, China, in late 2010 for the 16th Asian Games.

One of the highlights of the Games was a return to the top for **Liu Xiang**. At the 2008 Beijing Olympics, the superstar high hurdler was injured and couldn't do his best. It was a huge disappointment. However, he battled back after surgery, and at the Asian Games he took home the gold in the 110-meter race.

The Asian Games actually name a Most Valuable Player, an unusual award at such a large event. With two gold medals, badminton star **Lin Dan** from China took home the honor. In the race for most medals by a country, China, Japan, and South Korea headed the list. China's 416 medals were almost twice as many as Japan's, however. Happily, 35 of the 45 countries took home at least one medal.

Commonwealth Games

The British Commonwealth once controlled dozens of countries around the world. It was so large that it was said that "the sun never sets on the British Empire." Much has changed over the decades, though, and most of those countries are now independent. However, they continue to interact with one another as former British possessions. One way is the Commonwealth Games, held every four years.

The 2011 event took place in Delhi, India. More than 71 countries from every part of the globe sent teams to take part in more than 20 different sports. The Games featured a few sports that you won't see in the Olympics but that are popular in former British colonies. New Zealand won the netball event, while South Africa won three golds in lawn bowling.

Netball: No backboard!

FLYING FEET!
Thailand (in blue) captured the 2011 Sepak Takraw World Cup, defeating Malaysia in the final. This volleyball-like sport, played with feet instead of hands, is a big deal in Southeast Asia.

Baseball, football, basketball . . . boring ball! There's more to the world of sports than just the stuff you see on the TV highlights. This section takes a trip into the odd, bizarre, and unusual from around the world. From mud to marbles, this section has everything that just didn't fit anywhere else!

◀ Foot's Up!

In the action-packed sport of sepak takraw, acrobatic athletes use their feet to play a form of volleyball over a net that's five feet high! The three players on each team can spike and block like volleyball players, but upside down . . . and with their feet. The players use a plastic ball that's about as big as a softball but very flexible, so it doesn't hurt (too much!) when they whack it. Players have to be great leapers as well as very creative kickers.

▲ Everybody into the Mud!

Look like fun? Some people in Irvine, California, decided that the usual 5K race just wasn't muddy enough. So they added lots of water, and—splash!—they created the annual Irvine Lake Mud Run. Besides sloshing through gooey pits like this one, runners have to climb over slippery obstacles, crawl through smelly tubes, and clamber up sticky ramps. The winner is the fastest, however . . . not the dirtiest.

▲ Concrete Canoes

Check out the canoe in this picture. Looks pretty seaworthy, right? Cruising along on a river, these paddlers are racing their boat. What makes this very different from your average canoe is . . . this one is made from concrete! Engineering students use their math and design skills to make a canoe from a material that usually sinks like, well, concrete. This particular boat, from Cal Poly, San Luis Obispo, captured the national college championship. It not only floated, it won the final race.

Surf's Up . . . and Moving Fast! ▶

You've heard of regular surfing (check out the pro champs on page 132). Surfers hit the beaches of the world to ride waves big and small. But that's not the only place to surf. Daring riders also surf rivers! They look for places where bends or dips create steady wave faces. Instead of moving forward with the water, as in the ocean, river surfers basically stay in one place as the water whooshes under them.

Germany has several great river surfing spots, as does Canada. Oregon has a couple, and Colorado is also a popular spot. It's for experts only, however, so don't try this at home (even if your home is on a river!).

The Mascot with the Mostest

Since college teams get to be champions, it's only right that the mascots get a shot at glory, too. The Universal Cheerleaders Association held a mascot championship in Florida. Dozens of colorful mascots from schools around the country showed up to strut their stuff, including dance moves, comedy routines, and the ability to keep a giant foam head on for a long time. **Goldy the Gopher** from the University of Minnesota claimed top honors.

Odds . . . and Ends

- Stories like this one are why your mother always tells you to "be prepared." Pro tennis player **Bojana Jovanovski** set out from her home in Serbia for the Mercury Open. She landed in Carlsbad to find no one waiting for her. After asking around, she discovered that she was in Carlsbad, New Mexico. But the tennis event was in Carlsbad, California! She got some help and made it to the correct Carlsbad just in time for her first match . . . which she lost.
- A soccer goalie's job is to stop goals, not make them. But **David Bingham** of the San Jose Earthquakes paid no attention to that. A punt he made in a July 2011 game traveled 90 yards, bounced once . . . and went into his opponent's goal!
- Fans at a Los Angeles Angels game in May 2011 broke a world record for the largest gathering of people wearing costume masks. The team handed out 25,000 of the sparkly red masks, inspired by those worn by wrestlers in Mexico. ▶▶▶

- In the "too much time on your hands" department, a man named **John Bates** set a world record by bowling 850 perfect games on his Wii console.

Wacky Car Races ▶

NASCAR's got nothing on these creative daredevils. At wacky car races, held at many places around the world, people build bizarre rolling contraptions. They put them on a hill and . . . look out below! This weird rolling squirrel is from a race in Russia. Races are also held on the streets of Los Angeles and on beaches in Florida, among many other places.

▼ Record Race

At the 2011 London Marathon, more than 35,000 people ran the 26.2-mile course. Nothing special, right? Wrong. So many of them were dressed in odd costumes that the folks at Guinness World Records had a field day. Among the 34 records officially set at the race were marks for the fastest marathons run while dressed as a jester, a fairy, a policeman, a superhero, a gingerbread man, a Viking, and Mr. Potato Head.

A host of costumed characters completed the record-setting London Marathon.

Other records set on this very unusual day included most Rubik's Cubes solved while running a marathon (100), most people linked together running a marathon (47), and fastest marathon while carrying a 60-pound pack.

More importantly, the race set another record: most money raised for charity by a race. The runners got pledges that brought in more than $45 million to help others!

Not every sport makes you sweat. Here's a look at a few very unusual competitions that have winners and medals and rules . . . but don't really fit into the usual lineup of sports championships.

NO SHAVING!

Men who love their facial hair now have a way to earn gold medals. At the World Beard and Moustache Championships, hairy men from around the globe gather to let judges peer at their faces. The men spend months growing and grooming their fuzzy displays. At the event, they compete in categories that include Dali, Hungarian, musketeer, Verdi, Garibaldi, and of course, freestyle.

At the 2011 event, held in Norway, Germany led the way with eight gold medals, followed by the United States, the defending champion, with six. Germany's **Elmar Weisser** (at the center of the hair-raising picture) captured the award for best in show.

SKIP THIS!

Head off to Easdale Island, Scotland, if you think you've got what it takes to win the World Stone Skimming Championships. Held since 1983, the event pits skimmers from around the world. To win, you have to fling your stone the farthest while skipping it along the surface of the water down a line marked by buoys. The 2010 men's winner was local hero **Dougie Isaacs**, who zinged his stone more than 190 feet (58 meters)! The women's champ was Germany's **Manuela Kniebusch**.

MARBLES COUNTRY!

Both champions at the 88th annual National Marbles Tournament were from the same place: Allegheny County, Pennsylvania. That's girls' champ **Bailey Narr**, 11, getting congrats from boys' winner **Brandon Matchett**, 12.

THE MEGA-AWESOME SPORTS INTERNET LIST!

MAJOR SPORTS WEBSITES

These are the "Big Five" of professional sports leagues. Each of these websites includes links to the individual websites of the teams in the league, plus bios of top players, video clips, schedules of games, even how to find tickets!

Major League Baseball
mlb.mlb.com

National Hockey League
www.nhl.com

National Basketball Association
www.nba.com
www.wnba.com

Major League Soccer
www.mlssoccer.com

National Football League
www.nfl.com

Editor's Note for Parents and Teachers: These websites are for information purposes only and are not an endorsement of any program or organization over others. We've made every effort to include only websites that are appropriate for young sports fans, but the Internet is an ever-changing environment. There's no substitute for parental supervision, and we encourage everyone to surf smart . . . and safe!

OTHER SPORTS LEAGUES

Check out these websites for schedules, results, and info on athletes in your favorite sports featuring individual competitors.

Action Sports
www.allisports.com

Bowling
www.pba.com

Drag Racing
www.nhra.com

Golf
www.pgatour.com

www.lpga.com

Ice Skating

www.usfigure skating.org

IndyCar Racing

www.indycar.com

Motocross/ Supercross

www.supercross.com

Stock Car Racing

www.nascar.com

Surfing

www.aspworldtour.com

Tennis

www.wtatennis.com

COLLEGE SPORTS

Follow your favorite team's road to the football BCS championship or the basketball Final Four with these major college sports sites. You can find links to the schools that are members of these conferences.

Bowl Championship Series

www.bcsfootball.org

Atlantic Coast Conference

www.theacc.com

Big East Conference

www.bigeast.org

Big Ten Conference

www.bigten.org

Big 12 Conference

www.big12sports.com

Conference USA

conferenceusa .cstv.com

Mid-American Conference

www.mac-sports.com

Mountain West Conference

www.themwc.com

Pac-12 Conference

www.pac-12.org

Southeastern Conference

www.secsports.com

Sun Belt Conference

www.sunbeltsports.org

Western Athletic Conference

www.wacsports.com

National Collegiate Athletic Association

www.ncaa.com

This site features information about all the college sports championships at every level and division.

MAJOR SPORTS EVENTS

You'll find links to most big-time events—like the Super Bowl, the World Series, or the NBA Finals—on those sports' league websites. But here are several more world-wide sporting events that are worth a bookmark.

Little League World Series
www.littleleague.org/worldseries/index.html

The Masters
www.masters.com

Pan Am Games (2011)
www.guadalajara2011.org.mx/eng/01_inicio

Summer Olympics (2012)
www.london2012.com

Tour de France
www.letour.fr/us

Winter Olympics (2014)
sochi2014.com/en

World Cup (Soccer)
www.fifa.com/worldcup

X Games
espn.go.com/action/xgames

YOUTH SPORTS ORGANIZATIONS

Rather play than watch? These websites can help get you out on the field!

Baseball
www.littleleague.org

Basketball
www.njbl.org

Football
www.usafootball.com

Golf
www.juniorlinks.com

Ice Hockey
www.usajuniorhockey.com

Soccer
www.ayso.org

Tennis
www.usta.com

MEDIA SITES

If you're looking for the latest scores or news about your favorite sport, try some of these websites run by sports cable channels or sports publications.

CBS Sports
www.cbssports.com

ESPN
espn.go.com

FOX Sports
msn.foxsports.com

Sporting News Magazine
aol.sportingnews.com

Yahoo! Sports
sports.yahoo.com

SPORTS HISTORY

It seems like big fans know all there is to know about the history of their favorite sports. Learn more about yours at any of these websites that take you back in time.

Hickok Sports
www.hickoksports.com

Retrosheet (Baseball)
www.retrosheet.org

***Sports Illustrated* Vault**
sportsillustrated.cnn.com/vault

Sports Reference Family of Sites
www.baseball-reference.com

www.basketball-reference.com

www.pro-football-reference.com

www.hockey-reference.com

www.sports-reference.com/olympics

PLAYERS ASSOCIATIONS

You're probably a little young to think about making money playing a sport. But if you're interested in the business side of things or want to discover more about what it's like to be a pro athlete, these sites may help.

MLB Players Association
mlbplayers.mlb.com

NBA Players Association
www.nbpa.org

NFL Players Association
www.nflplayers.com

NHL Players' Association
www.nhlpa.com

MLS Players Union
www.mlsplayers.org

GAMES

Finally, check out these sites for some rainy-day sports fun and games on the computer.

www.nflrush.com

www.sikids.com

NCAA DIVISION I CHAMPS

MEN'S SPORTS
(2010–2011 School Year)

Akron's Zips were soccer's best.

BASEBALL
South Carolina

BASKETBALL
Connecticut

CROSS COUNTRY
Oklahoma State

FENCING (CO-ED TEAM)
Notre Dame

FOOTBALL (BCS)
Auburn

GOLF
Augusta State

GYMNASTICS
Stanford

ICE HOCKEY
Minnesota Duluth

LACROSSE
Virginia

RIFLE (CO-ED TEAM)
Kentucky

SKIING (CO-ED TEAM)
Colorado

SOCCER
Akron

SWIMMING AND DIVING
California

TENNIS
USC

TRACK AND FIELD (INDOOR)
Florida

TRACK AND FIELD (OUTDOOR)
Texas A&M

VOLLEYBALL
Ohio State

WATER POLO
USC

WRESTLING
Penn State

WOMEN'S SPORTS
(2010–2011 School Year)

BASKETBALL
Texas A&M

BOWLING
Maryland Eastern Shore

CROSS-COUNTRY
Villanova

FIELD HOCKEY
Maryland

GOLF
UCLA

GYMNASTICS
Alabama

ICE HOCKEY
Wisconsin

LACROSSE
Northwestern

ROWING
Brown

SOCCER
Notre Dame

SOFTBALL
Arizona State

SWIMMING AND DIVING
California

TENNIS
Florida

TRACK AND FIELD (INDOOR)
Oregon

TRACK AND FIELD (OUTDOOR)
Texas A&M

VOLLEYBALL
Penn State

WATER POLO
Stanford

The women from Brown rowed to their third national title in the last five years.

THE BIG EVENTS CALENDAR

September 2011

4 Cycling
Mountain Bike World Championships, final day, Champéry, Switzerland

8 NFL
Regular season begins

10–11 Tennis
U.S. Open final matches, New York, New York

10–17 Weight Lifting
World Championships, Paris, France

12–18 Wrestling
World Championships, Istanbul, Turkey

19–25 Gymnastics
World Rhythmic Gymnastics Championships, Montpellier, France

22–25 Golf
PGA Championship, Atlanta, Georgia

TBA* Basketball
WNBA Finals

Competitors at the World Rhythmic Gymnastics Championships exhibit athleticism and grace.

October 2011

TBA* **Baseball**
MLB postseason begins (League Division Series, League Championship Series, World Series)

8 **Swim/Bike/Run**
Ironman Triathlon World Championship, Kailua-Kona, Hawaii

8–16 **Gymnastics**
World Artistic Gymnastics Championships, Tokyo, Japan

November 2011

6 **Running**
New York City Marathon

15–20 **Golf**
Presidents Cup, Melbourne, Australia

20 **NASCAR**
Ford 400, final race of Chase for the Cup, Homestead, Florida

20 **Soccer**
MLS Cup, Carson, California

December 2011

2-3 **College Football**
ACC Championship, Tampa, Florida; Pac-12 Championship, site to be determined; SEC Championship, Atlanta, Georgia

4 **College Soccer**
Women's championship game, Raleigh, North Carolina

A 2.4-mile swim is only the first part of the grueling Ironman triathlon competition.

11 **College Soccer**
Men's championship game, Hoover, Alabama

January 2012

2 **College Football**
Rose Bowl, Pasadena, California

3 **College Football**
Sugar Bowl, New Orleans, Louisiana

4 **College Football**
Orange Bowl, Miami, Florida

5 **College Football**
Fiesta Bowl, Glendale, Arizona

7–8 **NFL**
Wild Card Play-off Weekend

9 **College Football**
Bowl Championship Series National Championship Game, New Orleans, Louisiana

14–15 **NFL**
Divisional Play-off Weekend

16–29 **Tennis**
Australian Open, Melbourne, Australia

John Velazquez rode Animal Kingdom to victory at the 2011 Kentucky Derby.

22 NFL
Conference championship games

22–29 Figure Skating
U.S. Figure Skating Championships, San Jose, California

26–29 Action Sports
Winter X Games 16, Aspen, Colorado

29 NFL
AFC–NFC Pro Bowl, Honolulu, Hawaii

February 2012

5 NFL
Super Bowl XLVI, Lucas Oil Stadium, Indianapolis, Indiana

26 NASCAR
Daytona 500, Daytona Beach, Florida

26 NBA
NBA All-Star Game, Orlando, Florida

March 2012

14–16 Action Sports
Winter X Games Europe 2012

26–Apr. 1 Figure Skating
World Figure Skating Championships, Nice, France

31–Apr. 2 Basketball
NCAA Men's Final Four, New Orleans, Louisiana

April 2012

1–3 Basketball
NCAA Women's Final Four, Denver, Colorado

5–8 Golf
The Masters, Augusta, Georgia

May 2012

5 Horse Racing
Kentucky Derby, Churchill Downs, Louisville, Kentucky

19 Horse Racing
Preakness Stakes, Pimlico Race Course, Baltimore, Maryland

27 Auto Racing
Indianapolis 500, Indianapolis, Indiana

June 2012

7–10 Golf
LPGA Championship, Henrietta and Pittsford, New York

9 Horse Racing
Belmont Stakes, Belmont Park, Elmont, New York

9–10 Tennis
French Open, final matches, Paris, France

TBA* Hockey
Stanley Cup finals begin

TBA* Basketball
NBA Finals begin

14–17 Golf
U.S. Open Championship, San Francisco, California

15 College Baseball
College World Series begins, Omaha, Nebraska

25 Tennis
All-England Championships at Wimbledon begin

30 Cycling
Tour de France begins, Liège, France

July 2012

5–8 Golf
U.S. Women's Open, Kohler, Wisconsin

10 Baseball
MLB All-Star Game, Kansas City, Missouri

19–22 Golf
British Open Championship, Lytham St. Annes, England

27–Aug.12 Summer Olympic Games
London, England

TBA* Action Sports
Summer X Games 18

August 2012

TBA* Baseball
Little League World Series, Williamsport, Pennsylvania

9–12 Golf
PGA Championship, Kiawah Island, South Carolina

Note: Dates and sites subject to change.

** TBA: To be announced. Actual dates of event not available at press time.*

Produced by Shoreline Publishing Group LLC
Santa Barbara, California
www.shorelinepublishing.com
President/Editorial Director: James Buckley, Jr.
Designed by Tom Carling, www.carlingdesign.com

The *Year in Sports* text was written by

James Buckley, Jr., and **Jim Gigliotti**

plus **Craig Zeichner** and **Zachary Vanderberg** (NHL).

Thanks to Brenda Murray, Stephanie Anderson, Chris Hernandez, Steve Scott, Esther Lin, and the all-stars at Scholastic for all their extra-inning and overtime help!

Photo research was done by the authors. Thanks to Steve Diamond of Scholastic Picture Services for his assistance in obtaining the photos.

Photography Credits

Front and back cover: All images courtesy of **Getty Images**.

Interior:
AP/Wide World: 8, 13, 18, 19 (inset), 20, 22, 23, 24, 25, 26 (2), 27, 28–29 (4), 30–31 (4), 32 bottom, 33, 34 top, 36, 37, 42–43 (3), 45, 47 (3), 48, 49 top, 50 bottom, 51 top, 59, 61 top, 62 bottom, 64 top, 65 top, 74, 76, 77 bottom, 78, 79 bottom, 80, 84 (2), 88 bottom, 89 bottom (2), 91 top, 94, 95, 101 top, 102 top, 102 bottom right, 103 bottom, 110–111 (2), 114 top, 121, 122, 124–125, 126 top, 127 bottom, 132 bottom, 139, 140, 144, 149 bottom, 152 (2), 153 bottom, 155 top, 156, 157, 161 bottom, 163, 167 bottom, 168, 169 top, 170 top, 172 bottom, 173 bottom, 175 top, 177, 179 top. **Getty Images:** 4–5, 9, 10, 11, 12, 14, 15, 16, 32 top, 34 bottom, 35 (2), 40, 44, 46, 49 bottom, 50 top, 51 bottom, 54, 56, 57, 58, 60, 61 bottom, 62 bottom, 63, 64 bottom, 65 bottom, 66, 67, 70, 71, 72, 75, 77 top, 79 top (2), 82, 85, 86–87 (3), 88 top, 89 top, 90 (3), 91 bottom (2), 92–93 (4), 96, 98, 99, 100, 101 bottom, 102 bottom left, 103 top, 104, 105, 107, 108, 112–113 (3), 114 bottom, 115 (2), 118, 120, 123, 126 bottom, 127 top, 128, 130, 132 top, 133, 134, 135, 136, 137, 138, 142, 143, 145, 146, 147, 151, 153 top, 154, 155 bottom, 158, 159, 160 (2), 161 top, 162, 164, 166, 167 top, 169 bottom, 170 bottom, 171, 172 top, 173 top, 174, 175 bottom, 176, 178 bottom, 179 bottom, 180–181 (3). **Cal Poly San Luis Obispo:** 178.